JAN 1 4 2015

D0770091

# When Life Hands You Alzheimer's, Make Aprons!

## A Daughter's Journal of Her Mother's Last Months

### Gwen O'Leary

authorHOUSE®

WILLARD LIBRARY, BATTLE CREEK, MI

AuthorHouse™
1663 Liberty Drive
Bloomington, IN 47403
www.authorhouse.com
Phone: 1-800-839-8640

Cover photograph by Lon R. Hinde
The author, using solar power, sewed the aprons
shown on the cover photograph.

© 2011 Gwen O'Leary. All rights reserved.

No part of this book may be reproduced, stored in
a retrieval system, or transmitted by any means
without the written permission of the author.

First published by AuthorHouse 4/22/2011

ISBN: 978-1-4567-5039-8 (e)
ISBN: 978-1-4567-5040-4 (sc)

Library of Congress Control Number: 2011906317

Printed in the United States of America

Any people depicted in stock imagery provided by Thinkstock are models,
and such images are being used for illustrative purposes only.
Certain stock imagery © Thinkstock.

This book is printed on acid-free paper.

Because of the dynamic nature of the Internet, any web addresses or
links contained in this book may have changed since publication and
may no longer be valid. The views expressed in this work are solely those
of the author and do not necessarily reflect the views of the publisher,
and the publisher hereby disclaims any responsibility for them.

I had the pleasure of serving as the primary care physician for Donna O'Leary. Gwen's book gives great insight into this sad condition that affects both the people afflicted by it and the caregivers. I have started recommending this book to the families of other patients of mine who have been diagnosed with Alzheimer's dementia.
—*Sindhu Kotwani, M.D.*

Gwen O'Leary's ability to find humor in the midst of heartbreak is refreshingly insightful and poignantly honest. Her writing style is both moving and poetic as she weaves her personal story of love, loss and bittersweet nostalgia. Readers will delight in O'Leary's visual imagery as she shares her encounter with the flip side of the parent/child relationship.
—*Connie Nelson, former editor, McGraw-Hill Publishing*

Gwen O'Leary's book is beautifully written, insightful, delicate, witty, direct, piercing, evocative, and wrenching. She has the ability to write about the awful without making it awful. O'Leary put it out there truthfully, warts and all, and emerged hopeful, grateful, whole and entire. What a lesson she and her mother have taught us all.
— *Grace Howaniec, former columnist, Milwaukee Journal Sentinel; former feature writer, Chicago Sun-Times states*

Although the subject of Alzheimer's can be a depressing subject, Gwen O'Leary's book is a joy to read. You can feel the frustration, enjoy the humor, and be touched by the sadness. As a caregiver, it made me realize that the person with Alzheimer's is still there, but lost in confusion. We need to remember to treat them with dignity and love. I am recommending, "When Life Hands You Alzheimer's, Make Aprons!" to all my co-workers and friends.
—*Maggie Corey R.N., B.S.*

Gwen O'Leary's personal account demonstrates that tragedy and humor can coexist in the same instant. As a psychotherapist having worked with families who struggle with the diagnosis of Alzheimer's I applaud O'Leary's writing. Her account of Alzheimer's mirrors the countless families I have seen. This book brings to light the myriad emotions felt by patients and families facing this disease.
—*Jeff Thompson MA, LPC*

# Author's Note

All of the events described in this book are true. I wrote what I experienced with my mother as she suffered the ravages of Alzheimer's. Historical family stories passed down to me were described as close as my memory allowed. These events are true; the people I wrote about are real people. With permission from every person mentioned in this book, I have used their given birth names.

I have attempted to remove from the book any offensive language, except where necessary, to convey the true meaning of a particular experience or phrase.

I've been to sorrow's kitchen
and licked clean all the pots.
—*Susan Straight*

~To Mom ~
Without You,
There Would Be No Story


~To Dad~
Who Always Appreciated
My Writing And My Humor
And Called Me His
*Pen Gwen*

## Young and Innocent

My parents, Gerald and Donna O'Leary, during their dating years. Mom was fifteen, Dad was eighteen. This picture is etched on their shared head stone at the Steckley Cemetery near Applegate, Michigan. On their head stone, the following phrase describes their lifelong love.

*Our Love For Each Other*
*Was A Journey*
*Starting At Forever*
*Ending At Never*

*Photo courtesy of the Katie Frostic collection*

# Table of Contents

Author's Note · vii

Back To The Beginning  (Prologue) · xv

1  Getting The Death Bed Ready · 1

2  "All The Way Back To My Fanny?" · 7

3  Napkins And Paper Clips · 13

4  Mom's Green Thumb · 20

5  The First Days Of The Last Five Months · 26

6  Tortured Omelet · 29

7  In The Land Of Hit And Miss Memory · 34

8  "Cookies? We Have Cookies!" · 38

9  I Would Rather Burst Into Flames · 46

10  Help Is Spelled H-e-r-b · 53

11  When Life Hands You Alzheimer's,
     Make Aprons! · 61

12  Are You Looking For Sympathy? · 67

13  Big Girl Panties · 73

14  "How Did You Find Me At That Place?" · 77

15  Hey! I'm Still Me In Here · 84

16  Grandma Fed Us Roadkill · 93

17  Music In My Toes · 98

18  You Were The Bravest                   105

19  Mom's Seventy-Fifth Birthday           110

20  Where's Gerald?                        116

21  Alzheimer's Last Gift                  122
        Looking Back                       127
        Farm Stories                       130

22  Bean Summer Mornings                   132

23  Riding Ollie                           138

24  Killdeer                               143

And Now A Round Of Applause For:           149

About The Author                           151

# Back To The Beginning
# (Prologue)

In April of 2007, my husband and I decided to sell our century old home in Salt Lake City. It required constant maintenance; we felt as if the house and yard owned us. We dreamed of a different life: one with less real estate responsibility. Our goal to live on the road in a 16-foot travel trailer became a reality when the house sold in August. Without a mortgage and a lifetime of accumulations, we simplified our life. A few tools, four handmade quilts and a sailboat stayed behind in storage. We pointed our compass west and said, "Let's go live a life." For three months, we climbed peaks in the Rockies, shivered under towering Redwoods, tickled our toes in the Pacific, and fell asleep listening to coyotes howl in the desert.

Then the call came with news concerning my dad's declining health. He was not treating his high blood pressure; he suffered from extensive edema, required a cane to walk, and had shortness of breath. We left the truck and trailer in Las Vegas and flew to Florida, thinking we could assist with Dad's health care: give him a pill or two, help with some daily chores, and maybe have time to watch the sunrise over the Atlantic. Oh, how simple it sounded.

We didn't do so well. Within a month, Dad was hospitalized with congestive heart failure. After a flurry of tests and doctor's consultations, we learned he had renal disease brought on by hypertension. The doctors mentioned *kidney dialysis*, which sounded like a freight train bounding down the tracks in our direction. Dad's hospitalization put Mom's long-standing dementia into a tailspin. Before we fully understood Dad's diagnosis and treatment options our suspicion that Mom suffered from Alzheimer's was finally confirmed. It was as if a giant foot came down and stepped on the brake pedal, and our short, sweet life on the road came to a screeching halt. We were living life differently, that's for sure. Just not the way we intended.

I left home at 17 to attend college. At age 20, I left Michigan and headed west to settle in Colorado. I was geographically and, quite honestly, emotionally severed from my family for 35 years. Suddenly I had parents again, very needy parents. My sister and I rarely connected over the years, but now we found ourselves in the same ball court as tag-team caregivers.

My husband Lon and I took the winter duty in Zephyrhills, Florida. During the summer months, Katie and her husband Del continued to look after them on their farm near Applegate, Michigan. Our parents, Donna and Gerald, could only give minimal aid to each other; in their stead, Sis and I became a replacement wife and husband for each of them. The shoes we decided to step into were large and clumsy. Kicking them off was not an option for us; we learned how to find comfort in the uncomfortable.

The following chapters are from a journal I kept during the winter of 2009-2010. Each chapter is part journal and part reflection on who my mom was, how Alzheimer's changed her, and how I learned to be a caregiver.

# 1

# Getting The Death Bed Ready

Our third winter as caregivers begins at the end of a six month, 18,000-mile journey to Alaska, across Canada to the Maritime Provinces and down the eastern seaboard to Mom and Dad's home in Zephyrhills, Florida. It was the trip of a lifetime. However, years of planning to see our country's last frontier was bittersweet as this may be the last year of my mother's life.

At every vista, curve in the road, and seductive blue swirl of glacial ice, I saw a country my grandfather and father longed to see. My eyes felt selfish, it was a venture they never made. I blogged my way across tundra, mountains and prairies, sending Dad every detail from Anchorage to Nova Scotia. Digital pictures arrived on my sister's computer and snail mail delivered maps to Dad so he could follow our trail.

While I traveled, my sister, Katie, struggled with the dynamics of Mom's accelerating Alzheimer's. Del, Katie's husband, took on many of the dialysis duties with Dad. I offered verbal support every few days from a crackling cell phone. It was a sorry substitute for a hug and the tangible assistance she needed.

By the time October arrived, I was road-weary and ready for my tour of duty and Katie hung by a thin thread. In early spring, Mom transferred a mild case of viral pink eye to Kate and Dad. For them it was a vicious case of pink eye that virtually blinded them through the month of May and into June. Viral pink eye runs its own course and debilitates the entire body. Katie describes it best:

> We kept curtains and blinds closed and wore clip-on sunglasses over regular sunglasses. What little light got through was incredibly painful. The whites of our eyes were pure red and looked like jelly. For a period of time, we felt like we had a hot needle going through the middle of our eye. Ice packs were too brutal on our tender eyelids and surrounding skin. We poured rice into well-worn socks and put them in the freezer, these cold packs helped soothe our throbbing eyes. My vision, for a period of 7-9 days, was like looking through Vaseline and walking through thick fog.

Mom didn't understand why everyone had red eyes and laid around so much, she kept herself busy lifting rice bags from everyone's eyes asking, "Do you really think this is helping?" Dad's poor eyes, red-rimmed and swollen, made Mom think he had applied makeup; she chastised him, "I know everyone has a different way of putting on eye make-up, but I really don't like how you put on yours."

In June, Del contracted the pink eye virus; he recovered from it just before he underwent surgery to replace both knees. Katie is a pillar of strength, and the support she received from a tight-knit farm community gave her the lifeline she needed. But things were unraveling fast. Through the summer, Mom was Katie's constant shadow. Dad was getting weaker. He spent non-dialysis days sleeping and recovering from the treatments and showed no interest in the farm activity that once provided him a source of entertainment. The last phone conversations between us, before I put my feet back on the Zephyrhills property, ended with Katie on the verge of tears and a quivering voice asking, "You are going to make it to Florida, right?"

The first call I made when I arrived in Zephyrhills was to a hospice organization. Before Mom arrived, I intended to interview and carefully select a support team that would assist me as I helped Mom die. Lon and I both attended to a myriad of details before Katie and Del arrived with our needy parents. Once they arrived, their high-octane medical needs would keep us swamped. My parents own two mobile homes, 25 feet apart from each other; in two weeks, I would be daughter, neighbor, and caregiver.

Hospice recommended getting a hospital bed in place before Mom arrived. Katie agreed it was a good idea, "She won't remember her bed," she reassured me. "She hasn't recognized *me* several times through the summer. Get rid of the queen bed, she'll never know." Kate reminded me that she had removed a sofa, coffee table, two end tables, and two lamps from my parents living quarters; Mom never noticed. How could she possibly remember one bed?

I'm prepared to spend many hours of tedium in Mom's room waiting for death to relieve her of a hideous disease. Murky gloom is not a decorating style I'm comfortable with, so the dark green curtains and bedspread went into storage. I lightened the room with crisp, white valances over the windows and hauled out a bright pastel, appliquéd quilt, which Katie had made over 40 years ago, to drape the bed. Mom hasn't slept in the bedroom for several years; her bed has been a reclining chair in the corner of their dining area. I'm curious about her response to the changes. Katie kept telling me not to worry, "You'll see soon enough for yourself how far she's slipped. She won't notice a thing."

Florida's summer heat and humidity creates a mustiness that hangs heavy in the air and clings to every surface. I pried open stubborn windows, washed anything that could fit in the washer, hauled mattresses out to soak in the sun and shampooed carpets. Mom's clothes hung sweet and ready in her closet, her room was bright and cheerful and fresh flowers on her hope chest and dresser awaited her arrival. All the details are reminiscent of the room I prepared 34 years ago for my son. I had often paused to peek in the nursery, caressing my swollen stomach, while anxiously anticipating the moment I would finally see a baby lying in the bassinet.

I found myself wondering what it would feel like to see my mother's body in the deathbed I'd prepared. I ran my hand over the appliquéd tulips; the cotton was worn and soft with age. I thought of her life well-lived and how much she had aged since diagnosis. Soon, very soon, I believed she would lay here, a withered lump under this old quilt.

Mom surprised us all. When they arrived from the

airport after an exhausting day of air travel, Mom turned into a chatterbox at the dinner table. "I'm so glad you managed to get dinner on the table. I tried to get someone to stop the car so I could buy some groceries," she tells us. "I knew everyone would be hungry, and I would need to cook." I look at Katie who's slowly shaking her head at me. I get the message; Mom is trying to act as if she has all her wits about her. She sees her family gathered, she was always in charge of the meals and she wants everyone to believe she's the same ol' Donna. I call it "speaking in script," when Mom does this, she sounds like a bad actress on a 1950's daytime soap opera. It's pitiful.

Mom's vitality stuns me; she is not the person Katie described during our many phone conversations. There were periods when Mom slept for several days, lost her appetite and took in few fluids. Katie often commented, "I think it's time to get hospice involved." Alzheimer's doesn't follow a nice linear pattern; Mom's symptoms seem to rise and fall like a schizophrenic tide. She could be down for a week and then suddenly come back to life in the form of an angry, wet cat, badly in need of a dry towel and a warm bowl of milk.

After dinner, Katie and I held our breath when Mom headed to her bedroom. We both followed, our apprehension building, as she got closer to her room. She walked in, took one look, and announced, "Someone stole my bed." I wanted to bonk my sister on the head. Now we had to come up with a quick excuse. "You can't sleep laying down, Mom, it makes you nervous, so we bought you a special bed," I grabbed the control and started pushing buttons. "See, the head of the bed can come up, so can the feet. It'll be like sleeping in your reclining chair."

"No, no, no, no, no," was her response. She wasn't buying my story. I tried to divert her attention to the fresh flowers. "Mom, look, did you see the flowers I bought? It's your homecoming gift. Does it feel good to be back?" Mom looked at me with surprise and laughed like the joke was on me. Then with perfect indignation she said, "We just went for a *drive*, I've only been gone for a couple of hours!"

She had just displayed a perfect example of how Alzheimer's has altered her brain. In the same moment she's cognizant of her stolen bed, she's unaware of the six months she spent in Michigan *and* a day of air travel. Katie and I looked at each other, our emotions as confused as Mom's brain. We could hold each other and sob or fall down laughing at the quirky Mommy we have acquired.

Before Katie returned to Michigan and left me in charge in Florida, she gave me an assignment. "Find something funny everyday," she advised, "it'll be easy to see the heartbreaking sadness, you're going to need to laugh if you want to survive."

I accepted the challenge—let's see how well I do.

# 2

# "All The Way Back To My Fanny?"

I was so naive and unprepared for the new equation Mom's disease would add to our daily routine.

**Urinary Incontinence + Alzheimer's =
Intimate Bathroom Encounters**

I threw away her underwear before she arrived in Florida this winter. Sis and I knew the move would cause, what we call, an "Alzheimer's tumble." Well-meaning friends warned, "You know the move to a different environment isn't good for your mom, it will make her Alzheimer's worse." True. But Mom has two homes and two daughters who are sharing the responsibility; Sis needs a break and nothing we do is ever going to make Mom's Alzheimer's *better*.

Many decisions require us to put *our* mental well-being and Dad's into consideration. We are all flying by the seat of our pants in an attempt to keep our marriages and lives intact as we speed down the destructive road Alzheimer's and Dad's kidney failure has created. It often feels as if Larry, Moe and Curley are at the wheel. We *expect* the change in environment will cause her to digress, so we are going to take advantage of it and move her from underwear to geriatric pull-ups. Just maybe she won't put up too much of a fight.

Mom is not happy about the conversion, "I'm not a baby," she tells me as I help guide her legs into the underwear. "Of course you're not, but it's hot here and you drink more, this is the underwear you wear in Florida." None of this is really a lie, and my matter-of-fact tone and attitude makes for a compliant Mommy.

"Whew!" I think, "That was easy." Both Sis and I have tussled with Mom about her underwear. Last winter she liked to wear two pairs: a regular panty with a urinary pad followed by a long-legged girdle. She was positive the girdle was good for a week—maybe even ten days (!) before it needed to visit the washing machine. I would often find dirty underwear in her drawer all nicely rolled up and fastened at each end with rubber bands. Sis and I called it "sausage underwear." I soon tired of unrolling and sniffing panties to find the soiled ones. To save my nose from the onslaught of ammonia, I tossed the whole lot into the washer, dirty or not. I enlisted Mom's help with the laundry; she loved to roll her clean panties into sausages, often commenting, "I wonder why I've used so many panties!"

I have furnished the bathroom with an arsenal of supplies for her: feminine soap and powder, big wet wipes, little wet wipes, plenty of washcloths and hand towels, and a drawer full of adult pull-ups. For me, I have rubber gloves, air freshener, and a very expensive jug of hand sanitizer in a lotion formula. There is room for a large wastebasket to house all the soaked items and I've added a supply of plastic grocery bags to put the pull-ups in before they land in the wastebasket. I've searched the medical supply stores for a supersized-diaper genie; it hasn't hit the geriatric market yet. The toilet booster seat, supplied by hospice, completes the ensemble.

All this collides with the large, power-jet spa tub Dad installed for Mom when they bought this place. Mom once took long bubble baths and soaked in it after working in the yard. Now we don't allow our parents near this deep, slippery, white hole for fear we might never get them out. Tubs are taboo for people in their condition. The only thing the tub's good for now is the spigot. It is located near the toilet and easy for me to reach when I wet a washcloth and hand it to Mom. She is still able to keep herself clean if I do all the instructing.

Her poor hearing and lack of cognition makes for interesting bathroom conversation. I will hand her a nice, warm, sudsy cloth and say, "Ok, clean yourself between your legs."

"My face?" She asks.

"No, Mom, between your legs."

I speak loudly, carefully, enunciating each word, and look at her while I'm speaking. She finally understands and proceeds to clean herself and then asks, "Should I get all the way back to my fanny?"

"Yep, Mom, get all the way back to your fanny."

"My front fanny first?"

"Uh-huh, your front fanny first."

"Then my back fanny?"

"Yep, then your back fanny."

After she's done, I rinse, hand the cloth back and say, "Ok, now wipe away the soap."

"Wash my face?" She asks.

You get the picture.

We "front fanny, back fanny" ourselves through the routine every morning, if not several times a day.

Mom's home health aide arrives twice a week. She's very thorough and keeps a watchful eye on all Mom's parts for pressure sores, skin outbreaks, and cracks and crevices I haven't cleaned well enough. She goes after the dirt under Mom's fingernails and instructs me to clip her toenails. It's as if I get a report card twice a week. This is a good thing, since the responsibility of caring for two other bodies besides my own is a little overwhelming. It dawns on me that I am in charge of earwax, toe cuticles, and all points in between. I think to myself, "It's like caring for overweight twins who are just learning how to walk."

Mom keeps me entertained during our endless, intimate bathroom visits. She watched warily one day as I used a new pump cleanser that spurted soap onto the cloth in a foam. While wiping herself, she looked at me and announced rather disgustedly, "Something's fuzzy in my butt!"

She lies to me when I instruct her to brush her teeth, "I already brushed my teeth," she tells me.

"I didn't see you brush your teeth."

"Well, I did it when you weren't looking," she retorts.

Alzheimer's saps my creative energy. Either I'm searching for a way to trick her into doing something or I'm trying to find a clever way to direct her through daily routines. I've added my toothbrush to their bathroom cabinet, because if we're both brushing she doesn't put up a fight and I don't have to listen to, "Is this long enough?" every five seconds. She'll brush as long as I do without complaint.

I've moved a large juice pitcher from the kitchen to the bathroom; it works well as a rinsing device after Mom has swabbed herself with, "something fuzzy." I fill it with warm water then tell her to spread her legs and while she's still on the toilet I create a waterfall over her "front fanny," then by instructing her to lean forward I get the "back fanny" rinsed. When she sees me fill the pitcher she asks, "Is it time for the waterfall?"

When we're done with "fannies" and teeth, we have a face routine that brings back the Mom I had years ago. I warm the washcloth with hot water, add a mild face cleanser, and then instruct her to wash her face. She is slow and thoughtful as she carefully caresses her cheeks and chin with the cloth, then moves up to her forehead. Holding her hair back with one hand, she rubs on her furrowed brow. She stares at herself in the mirror with a look of recognition, as if the woman in the mirror is an old, thoughtful friend. She sighs heavily when she's done, as if she knows no amount of caressing will ever bring back the woman she was.

I take the cloth and hold her hand as I pump face lotion on her finger. "Where should I put this?" she asks. It's the same question every morning and every night. "Rub it into your face, Mom." She begins another thoughtful session of face caressing; she's calm and meditative as she works the lotion over her cheeks and nose. She peers into the mirror as if she's reading an old, worn map; fingers work the lotion into a lifetime of lines and age spots.

I stand and watch, transported back to our life on the farm. She would come in from the fields and head to the bathroom for a quick sink bath before rushing into town for groceries. Her lotions, creams, and perfumes sat near the mirror and I can remember watching her as she moisturized her skin and then tidied her hair before heading out into public.

When she's done spreading her lotion, she looks at me with tired eyes, "I'm ready for my chair," she tells me.

"We have to do your hair. Sit here and I'll get it styled really quick and then you can go to your chair." She watches as I section her hair and roll it with a curling iron.

"Do you know what you're doing?" she asks. She never trusts me with her hair.

"I do your hair everyday Mom, and everyone always says how nice you look."

"Well," she retorts, "don't take all the credit, it's my hair."

After I comb out her hair, I fasten three tiny clips in the back. She has thick, wavy, gorgeous hair; hair a teenager would covet, hair that I would love. "Get me a mirror so I can see the back," she demands. She scrutinizes my work as if she's headed to the prom, tilting this way, peeking that way, then looks at me and asks, "Where's my rouge?" After stroking a light dose of rouge, I hand her a tube of lipstick. When she's done pressing her lips together she looks at herself, then me. My knees buckle at her next comment.

"I wish I were as beautiful as you."

# 3

# Napkins And Paper Clips

Last winter Mom's most disgusting habit was saving restaurant napkins. After eating, she would use her long fingernails to scrape chunks of food from her napkin, then painstakingly match up the corners, carefully crease the folds and tuck it in her pocket as if it were a treasure map. It was painful to watch. We would all sit around the table and pretend it wasn't happening. To stop her was futile.

A cluster of old and new napkins filled every nook and cranny in their car. Some would make their way into the house where they gathered in drawers, cupboards, on the coffee table, and in between couch pillows. Pick up a magazine or book to read and neatly pressed between the pages were Mom's used napkins where dried bits of food glued them in place.

Mom resented and fought any trespass into her private domain, so Lon and I would sneak over to search their home when Dad took Mom out to eat. We felt part-burglar and part-Sherlock Holmes as we poked in cupboards, closets, and drawers for the macabre and unusual. We called it *"Geriatric Espionage."* Arming ourselves with garbage bags and rubber gloves, we swiftly walked through the house, opening drawers and cupboards in search of her hoarded napkins.

Napkins were not the only thing she saved. Used foam containers along with paper and plastic plates would find their way back into cupboards and drawers. Sometimes Mom had washed them well; even the cheapest of paper plates had a good dousing in the sink. We would find them limp and battered, all the little rippled edges flattened out from the scrubbing she gave them. Next to the washed paper plates, we would find plastic plates with crusted food, foam containers full of food and, sometimes, just food—like limp broccoli stems snuggling up next to the forks and spoons.

Mom's favorite breakfast spot, Sugar Shack, provides small plastic-covered containers for the brown sugar and raisins that come with an order of oatmeal. She had an admirable collection. They were cute and handy, didn't take up much space, and as quickly as we whittled down the supply to a manageable dozen she would cart more home and build a new stash.

She's not saving napkins this winter, she's not picking the foam containers out of the trash to wash, and the car is free of napkin clusters. This winter she's just saving her tissues. My husband and I watched in horror one day when, after blowing her nose, she laid the tissue carefully on the quilt stand to dry.

"Ah, maybe we should just throw that away," I suggested. She came back with, "No, I like to dry them out and reuse them."

"Ah, geez," I muttered, "It's going to be a long winter."

I shudder at every tissue that's been 'hung out to dry.' Like the napkin pathology, it's futile to ask her to stop. She won't remember the conversation, and she won't remember *not* to do it. Asking her to stop caused a thunderstorm of emotions.

Our conversation went like this:

"Mom, please don't save these tissues. They're covered with germs."

Her brown eyes drill into my begging blue, "Is this my house?"

"Yes," I heavily sigh and hang my head like a whipped puppy, "this is your house, but you need to throw these tissues away."

Again, brown eyes drill into blue. "Am I your mother?"

"Yes."

"Then go home to your house and leave me alone."

You see? Nothing but hard feelings and bruised hearts come out of such conversations.

I am disgusted with Mom's habit and revolted when I catch myself sticking a used tissue in my pocket for future use. I rip up my napkins at restaurants as soon as I'm done eating because I too have found myself unconsciously folding them as if each one were a *Magna Carta* deserving historic preservation. In the middle of a napkin-folding event, I have stopped myself, looked at my husband, who is warily watching me, and immediately crumpled it up in a ball as we both laughed at the genetic habit.

Some of Mom's habits make me feel like we come from backward hill country. I wonder how much more my husband can take. The tissue thing was bad, but now she's throwing food out into the back yard. In the middle of a meal, she will slowly push herself away from the table and start a slow shuffle towards the back porch.

"Ah…Mom, where are you headed?"

She holds up a greasy chicken leg and responds, "I'm going to throw this out to the cats."

"Mom, we don't have cats, just throw it in the trash."

"Well, the birds will pick at it then."

My husband slowly puts down his fork, looks at me with big eyes and raised eyebrows. I try to explain, "She thinks she's back on the Michigan farm."

"So," he calmly asks, "did you throw all your food garbage into the back yard?"

I'm thinking it's a good thing we are well into an established seventeen-year relationship and this is not a first date.

"Well no," I carefully explain, "we didn't exactly throw it into the backyard, but we did hurl as much as we could *across* the backyard and into the field."

I have vivid memories of the contests we would have with watermelon rinds. They were like flinging biodegradable boomerangs. Pitch them just right and they would sail over the sheets, waving in the breeze on the clothesline, then whiz above the raspberry hedge before landing in the bean field where they would start to decompose. In the spring, we plowed our compost heap into the soil.

My husband, who only visited his granddad's farm for a few weeks in the summer, came from a military family. He lived in sterile military houses stacked next to each other in suffocating rows. There was no chucking melon rinds to the field or flinging chicken bones to the cats in his childhood. He's getting a good dose of it now; whenever he mows the Florida yard, he finds eggshells, half-eaten sandwiches, and rigid toast that Mom brings home from restaurants. When we pick up decaying fruit under the orange and grapefruit trees, we gather up Mom's toss outs. It's one of the many peculiar chores in our care-giving package.

We watch Mom closely because she likes to hide the hot food delivered by Meals on Wheels. Two days after delivery, we may find it in the pantry behind the canned goods. Last winter, in this same pantry, I found a used urinary pad stuck to the cutting board. My sister and I share the bizarre experiences we have with Mom. It's as if we have a contest to see who comes across the most outrageous or funny. After telling Kate about the pad on the cutting board, she was dead silent. Then she said in a small voice, "You're making this up, right?

"Katie," I answered, "you can't make this stuff up."

I have found old funeral programs tucked under the hand soap in the bathroom. The dustpan took up residence in the dryer, and peanut butter ended up next to the screwdrivers in Dad's shop. Well, maybe we can't blame Mom for that one. Dad does like peanut butter. I often found my Easter basket in odd places; one year it was in the dryer. So as I search the house, I pretend its Easter and I'm looking for colored eggs. Otherwise, you could just weep over how fried her brain is.

Mom has a thing about writing little notes on all sorts of items. I dug through her lingerie drawer one day to determine her bra size. I found all of her bras and panties in a neat roll with a rubber band securing each end. After unrolling a bra, I looked at the limp, worn tag for a size, but only found Mom's tiny penmanship. She had carefully written, "Old, worn out, no elastic, throw away." I discovered her note on a spray-cleaning bottle that said, "Works Like Shit." Sure enough it did; I threw it away. "Works Like Shit," was a note that Mom wrote on many household items. Katie saved such a note, taped to a small nail clipper that apparently frustrated Mom. It's a prop she intends to use when she teaches classes on caring for patients with Alzheimer's. For that purpose, I'm sure it will work just fine.

Mom keeps the white tablets that Dad uses to get rid of roaches in the little containers she brings home from Sugar Shack. On the lid, in fine-point magic marker, she drew a picture of a roach. No notes, just a picture, a pretty good picture actually.

Somewhere in the process of trying to keep herself together while her brain took a beating from Alzheimer's, Mom fell in love with paper clips. A bill, a check to pay it, and the associated envelope could have as many as twenty paper clips attached in a painstaking but artful design. Birthday cards and letters were paper-clipped to each other, as were church bulletins and graduation announcements.

I found drawers that were full of unpaid bills attached to anything she could manage to clip together. If twenty paper clips couldn't do the job, she enlisted the elasticity of a dozen rubber bands to keep her life from unraveling. Katie unscrambled the paper clips and rubber bands in their Michigan residence, while I unclipped reams of paper in Florida. Between the two of us, we organized a snarl of papers. In the process, we discovered Mom made future payments to five different magazine subscriptions, some through the year 2013.

We keep Mom away from the bills, the checkbook,

and the paper clips. My sister will often send me clippings from my hometown newspaper; she may add an article, which my nephew Matt has written, or pictures of her granddaughters; as a standing joke, she attaches everything with numerous paper clips. I'm always searching for designer paper clips to send back to her. It's our way of getting a laugh out of the wacky and weird phenomena that Alzheimer's has brought to our lives.

We've promised never to exchange used tissues.

# 4

# Mom's Green Thumb

Alzheimer's has robbed my mother of her beloved gardening hobby. It was a pastime she labored at with love. Now the garden only frustrates her. She doesn't want me tending to her flowerbeds, but she still wants weeds pulled and flowers blooming. If I encourage her to come out with me and give her a few simple tasks, she trudges along reluctantly, pokes about her flowerbeds in confusion and in a few minutes finds Dad to announce, "This place is too much work, we need to sell it and get out."

In Sanilac County, Michigan, half a mile south of M46, between the farming communities of Carsonville and Sandusky, my parents owned 140 acres of rich farmland. Mom and Dad turned the shack on the property into a home and then Mom began to transform the yard. Tulips, daffodils, lilacs, and iris surrounded our lawn with blooms and fragrance in the spring. A bouquet from the garden would often sit on the piano or kitchen table. She bought petunias by the dozens to add splashes of color to the rock garden she created from an unsightly pile of rocks in the corner of the yard. The pile was there when they bought the farm in the late 50's. Since many were too big for her to move, she rearranged smaller rocks, added wheelbarrows of rich soil and created a remarkable flower garden where blooms poked their colorful faces around various rock shapes.

Long before water features became vogue, she excavated a miniature pond and added a little waterfall where the burble of water added charm to our farmyard. Ducks and chickens waddled and poked around our yard, which was bordered by pink peonies, raspberry bushes, and a strawberry patch. Had you taken a morning stroll through our yard, you were likely to spot a rabbit nestled under various blooming shrubs. Along Dad's work shed, three cherry trees produced beautiful, wedding-white flowers in the spring. By summer, shiny, red cherries studded the trees. If we were quicker than the birds that stripped the trees clean, we would make tart cherry pies.

Something was always blooming; Mom added plants and flowers by exchanging seeds and plants with friends and family as compulsively as boys exchange baseball cards. Johnny-jump-ups from Grandma's garden in Saginaw made their way to Mom's Sandusky yard. When my sister married and started her garden near the quaint village of Applegate, she transplanted Johnny-jump-ups from Mom's yard to hers. After a visit to her sister's home in Bay City, Mom would head home with a poppy, peony, or iris from Aunt Bertie's yard and a cake recipe from the kitchen.

When my father retired from General Motors, they sold their farm, and bought a home in Steamboat Springs,

Colorado. Mom immediately started to transform a barren piece of ground into a showpiece, which everyone admired for the flowerbeds and abundance of trees. She even took on the gardening responsibilities at the ski condominium where she worked as Head Housekeeper. Mom transformed the sedate condominium lobby into a colorful area by adding huge barrels of bright-red geraniums that greeted the guests on arrival. Each time I went to visit, more flowers graced the landscape around their yard and the terrain around the condominium. She had little patience with her employees who, not knowing the difference between a weed and a flower, pulled out an unblooming flower from her flowerbeds. My parents enjoyed twenty years in Steamboat Springs before officially retiring. Dad loved the mountains, but my mom wanted to be near family. So they sold their home in Colorado and headed to Florida where all Mom's brothers and sisters wintered.

Once again, Mom started transforming the yard, but, by this time, Alzheimer's was eating away at her brain. After a couple years, the yard was an ugly, overgrown mess. She gave no thought to how big something might grow; there was no symmetry or artistic qualities in her garden designs. Then she lost the physical ability to keep up with all the work a tropical garden requires.

By the time my husband and I arrived on the doorstep of Alzheimer's to assist as caregivers, the yard was a disaster. We had to hire a professional company to whack through the jungle. Mom no longer has a show-stopping yard. Her Florida yard is boring, but easy to manage. She still asks for marigolds in a little flowerbed near the front door; I plant marigolds and add pots filled with colorful flowers on the porches and patios for her to enjoy. Last winter, when I begged her to let me put bark or stones in a large, empty flowerbed to help cut down on weeding, she threw a tantrum like a two year old. As we stood in the yard, she yelled for all the neighbors to hear, "This is my yard; everyone is making decisions about my yard. I'm not in charge of anything anymore. Get out of my yard and leave me alone!" I let her win and spent five months weeding a flowerless flowerbed.

She's right; we are making decisions for her. In an attempt to make her feel as if she *is* in control, they haven't come soon enough. It's been difficult to decide when to step in and take things away like driving privileges. Or using the gas stove. It's hard to hear her beg for her independence, "...but it's my car, it's my kitchen, it's my yard." While Alzheimer's chips away at her brain from the inside, we chip away at her independence from the outside. Both are killing her. Taking away her independence is like locking her in a straight jacket.

This winter I managed to convince her to let me put some seeds into the empty flowerbed that I weeded last winter. "Mom, if I'm going to weed, I might as well be weeding around vegetables." She went with me to the store to get seeds and was incredulous about the idea. "You're going to plant a garden?" She acts as if I'm flying to the moon. She firmly states she wants no part of the work.

Maybe she can remember how much work a garden can be. Her farm garden produced vegetables not just by bushels and pecks; honestly, Mom grew tomatoes by the truckloads. She gave red, juicy tomatoes away as readily as she passed out Johnny-jump-ups.

Mom would wrestle and manhandle the powerful tiller up and down the garden getting it ready for spring planting. She pounded stakes at the end of each row, tied a string to each stake, then planted vegetables in rows as neat as lined paper. Mom planned our farm suppers around the vegetables she harvested from the garden. We dined on beans, peas, radishes, potatoes, tomatoes, and green peppers. However, the sweet corn she produced was the crème de la crème. We waited until the water boiled before heading to the cornrows to rip off fat ears of corn. We had corn so fresh it was like eating candy on a cob. Our family of six could easily eat through two dozen ears in one sitting. The stick of butter in the butter dish had a perpetual imprint of corn kernels throughout harvest time.

The bounty that came out of that garden plot fed us through cold Michigan winters and by the time the last canning jar came out of storage, another crop was ripening and Mom would start to stock up on a new stack of Ball canning lids.

My rows are not quite so neat but straight enough, it's a garden not so much for vegetables but for remembrances. A garden just for the joy of watching as a seed pokes its way towards the sun. I have not had a vegetable garden for several decades, so I'm like a little kid when just five days after planting, I spy a few tiny sprouts. I run in to get Mom and lead her along a path to the garden. "Oh, look. See there," she points to a slight linear rise in the soil. "See that little hump, that's where the seeds haven't quite broke through the soil, by tomorrow you'll see sprouts." She looks at the plot and smiles; I hope it helps her remember her gardens. But I don't ask. I just bask in the moment, take a deep sigh, and feel relieved that she hasn't demanded I plow it under.

She likes the little garden and can check on it by

peeking out her kitchen window. My garden is ever so humble, a mere drop of chlorophyll compared to what her green thumb produced. I may not get any vegetables; my garden may only produce smiles and a bit of joy—but it's a harvest worth preserving in my heart forever.

# 5

# The First Days
# Of The
# Last Five Months

*This journal entry is in its raw form. Writing has always been cathartic for me; it soothes my soul and calms my troubled brain. I wrote this early one morning after I had tossed and turned all night, struggling with anger and frustration. The rage flooded out of my brain into my fingertips. When Lon awoke, I read it to him. My voice cracked with emotion; reading it was as liberating as writing it. When I finished reading and looked at Lon, his eyes were wide, "Well," he said, "Feel better?" Indeed, I did and from that morning on, I swept past deeds under the bridge, put on the best "Gwen skin" I could muster. I only recall one more incident when I asked Lon to step in my shoes and give me an hour of respite. I have decided to keep this in its original form and resist the temptation to rewrite it and make myself sound less pathetic.*

My mother is a spoiled brat, a five foot two, 154 pound, hedonistic child, who stamps her foot and pouts when she doesn't get her way. It's a d___ good thing she has a serious brain disease or I would pack my bags and be on with my life.

Alzheimer's brings out the worst in her. Her new and unimproved gray matter exacerbates her attitude that 'her way is the only way.' I want a sweet and gentle mommy who doesn't throw a temper tantrum; I want a mommy who is kind and attentive to my weak and frail daddy. I want a daddy who's emotionally strong enough to tell her to shut up and go sit in a corner.

I'm sick of being patient with her disease; I'm weary of sorting out what is disease and what isn't and then acting appropriately. I'm tired of acting appropriately. I want to stamp my foot and get my way once and a while. I want to yell at them both and ask:

"Why didn't you take better care of yourselves? Why did you choose this hellhole of a trailer park? Of all the wonderful places you could have bought, places with swimming pools, activity centers, and exercise rooms, why, *why* did you choose this dive? Why didn't you stay active, keep your weight down, and take your blood pressure medicine? Why, when this was going to be your final home, the place you would grow old in, why did you buy a place with so many steps? Why did you install a deep and dangerous spa tub instead of a large walk-in shower? All that money you had and you didn't think to put any away for elderly care. What the h___ were you thinking?"

I know the answer to most of those questions and it all boils down to it's what my mother wanted and "what mommy wants, mommy gets, cause daddy doesn't have a back bone."

It's been a s___ two days of being a caregiver and I need a stiff drink.

# 6

# Tortured Omelet

My morning begins with an early wake-up call for Dad; he has fasting blood work at 8:50. The aging process and his declining health have made morning routines challenging. Some mornings it's as if I have a couple of toddlers to manage. Dad will fall asleep sitting on the bedside, so he requires constant prodding. Getting a pair of socks on wears him out, so he rests between putting on his socks, pants, and shirt. I check to make sure he's awake and making progress as I guide Mom to the bathroom for a pair of clean adult pull-ups.

Some days she surprises me and will be dressed by 7:00 a.m.; however, she will have on wet underwear and a dress skirt matched with one of Dad's western shirts. If I lay out clothes for her to wear, sometime in the middle of the night she manages to hang them back in the closet. She brushes her teeth with direction, but I am the one who styles her hair and tinges her cheeks with rouge.

She still manages to get a good slick of lipstick on; even without a mirror, she can deftly paint her lips.

I have just enough time to get my teeth brushed, but I use a ball cap for a hairdo. It's not everyday that I can get two faces and two hairdos ready for the day. Mom always looks very nice, even though I often look rough around the edges. I think of it as a compliment to me when people comment on how well she looks.

Florida is having a cold snap, so we've covered all our herbs, vegetables, and flowers as the temperatures have dipped to 33 degrees Fahrenheit. I start their car to get it warmed up and turn on the seat heaters. Dad heads to the car like a rusted, bent-over Tin Man and Mom toddles behind with a dazed expression as if she's just come back from Oz—minus the ruby slippers. It's hideous to watch my parents in the depths of feebleness; they are disassembling before my eyes. The cold weather makes them look even more pathetic, even with the car heated and the seats warmed they both sit in quiet, huddled bundles as I drive them to the doctor's office.

We could be in for a 30-minute wait, so I packed breakfast snacks for both of them. If the doctor's office is running behind, we may be driving Dad directly to physical therapy and he will need some nourishment to get him through a grueling 45-minute therapy session. All of this thinking ahead and planning is reminiscent of my life when raising children. Drinks, snacks, and extra clean clothes are all part of the adult diaper bag I keep supplied in the car.

We are in luck: Dad is out of the office by 9:05, so we have time to get home and have a leisurely breakfast before we head out again. As we pull in the driveway,

Mom wants to know, "What's to eat?" Since we have plenty of time, I suggest an omelet.

"OK, I'll help you."

I take a deep breath and steady myself for what is about to take place. As soon as we get in the kitchen, it starts up.

"How can I help?"

"Get the butter out of the fridge and put a tablespoon in the pan on the stove."

"What?"

"Go to the fridge and get the butter."

She comes to the counter with the butter and asks, "What should I do with the butter?"

"Put some in the pan on the stove."

Then, I notice she has left the fridge door open, "Mom, you left the door open."

She walks over to close it and asks as she stands staring into it, "Where's the butter?"

"It's here on the counter."

She comes back to the counter, stares at the butter and asks, "What should I do with it?"

"Put some in the pan."

"How much?"

"Oh, about a tablespoon."

"Is this a tablespoon?"

"Yep, that's good."

"Where should I put it?"

"It goes in the pan."

"What pan?"

"The pan on the stove."

I manage this conversation all the while calmly chopping onions, mushrooms, and chicken for their omelet.

She hovers next to me as I break the eggs. It's as if the umbilical cord is reattached. She is my little shadow, I'm her ray of sunshine. I remember the phrase she always used on us kids, "You kids are going to drive me to Wahjamega!" Other mothers would say something like, "You're going to drive me nuts." When we would visit relatives near Saginaw, we sometimes took a route through a town that had a mental institution. The town's name? Wahjamega. My Mom's family was very German and still used a few German phrases, so I assumed Wahjamega was a German name for crazy. This morning I wish I could commit either her or *myself* to Wahjamega.

With a bit of testiness in my voice I ask "Mom, why don't you put some toast in the toaster?" Anything to get her detached from my side.

She's sharp enough to catch my error and retorts, "Don't you mean put some *bread* in the toaster to toast?"

"Yup, you're right, put some *bread* in the toaster."

"Should I put this heel in, this thick piece?"

"Sure, go ahead, if you like the heel, that's great."

I try to stay chipper and not let the endless questions get to me. A mere 15 seconds pass before I hear her ask "What should I do with this?" I turn to look: she's holding two slices of bread, her head is ten inches from the under-counter, toaster oven.

"Go ahead and put it in the toaster."

"Where's the toaster?"

"My gosh," I think, "This would be funny if I weren't so in charge."

All the while Dad sits at the table reading the paper; he appears oblivious to the effort that it is taking to create a simple breakfast. He's buried his head in some sort of reading material from the minute he first learned to read. It's been his lifelong escape mechanism. His sister Eileen tells the story of him tending to baby sister Maureen. He would sit on the steps of the living room reading and would give Maureen's carriage a push with his foot. It would glide all the way through the dining room and into the kitchen where upon hitting the refrigerator, baby and carriage would come back to Gerald's waiting foot while his nose remained firmly planted in his book.

It would be great if he would help by engaging Mom and get her detached from me, but I let him stay in escape mode. It's why I'm here; I understand why he enjoys having me around to tend to both their needs. After several years of managing Mom alone, he needs a break from her weary disease.

I get Mom seated and bring the food to the table; she looks at the two slices of bread and announces, "I don't want toast."

"Well Mom, why did you toast two pieces of bread?"

"I didn't make toast," she answers.

I should know better than to ask "why?" Asking "Why?" and "Do you remember?" are ridiculous questions to ask an Alzheimer's victim.

My goal is to find something funny about Alzheimer's every day. With mornings like this, it's an easy assignment.

# 7

# In The Land Of
# Hit And Miss Memory

Mom is in the front seat, quiet as a church mouse, as I sit behind the wheel waiting for the light to change. In a driving daze, I'm exhausted, eager to get home, put her in her chair, and escape from caregiver mode for an hour. Just an hour is all I ask. Suddenly, Mom says, "Pittsburg, Pittsburg Steelers."

I slowly turn and look at her, "What?"

"The car ahead," she points. "It has Pittsburg on the bumper sticker. Steelers are a football team. Right?"

I don't see the word "Steeler's" anywhere on the bumper sticker. She has come up with this on her own. It amazes me she can come up with "Pittsburg Steelers."

Our family didn't watch or actively engage in playing sports—unless you count lawn croquet as a sport. How does she suddenly remember the name of a football team? When I was growing up, she rarely read a major newspaper and was not a morning or evening news junkie. I could bet on Grandma's grave she never sat through an entire football game, live or on television. Alzheimer's is merciless; the demon in her brain grants her a dose of sports memorabilia, but does not supply her with the name of her youngest great granddaughter.

I'm grateful for the hour of rest I get before I hear Mom knocking at my door. It's not a simple *knock-knock-knock*. She raps the entire time it takes us to get to the door. If we aren't answering soon enough, she'll start yelling in a pitiful voice, "It's Mom!" She sounds just like a little kitty left out in the rain.

Although it frustrates both Lon and me, we are lucky to have our own private abode. Under my sister's care in Michigan, my parents lived in Katie and Del's farm home. Mom loved to walk around the oak table in Katie's dining area. It was soothing for her; many Alzheimer's victims are calmed by walking repeatedly in a circle. Wearing dress shoes, Mom clomped on the wood floor and traveled many miles around the table throughout the summer.

Every few steps, her ill-fitting hearing aid would let off an annoying *Beep*. Del was recuperating from replacement surgery on both knees in a hospital bed located in the living room just off from the dining room. A man known for his incredible patience was brought to the brink of exasperation listening to Mom's Clomp - Clomp - *Beep*, Clomp - Clomp - *Beep*. Del's doctor dubbed him the Poster Man for double knee replacement given Del's unremitting dedication to all phases of recovery. Del was confined to bed and strapped to a continuous motion machine that provided range of motion. The machine brought one knee to his chest and pulled the other leg out straight; back and forth went Del's legs four hours a day. While strapped to the machine with one knee to his chest and the other leg pointing straight, Mom leaned over Del and asked, "Why aren't you out of bed and working?" Del is well known for his inability to sit still; he is a passionate farmer who loves being outdoors and cannot tolerate idleness. To be a prisoner in his own home, hooked to a machine, while living with a *Beeping,* Clomping mother-in-law—well, it was just about enough to undo a man.

When Mom tired of circling the table, she would head out to find Sis. "Kaaa Tee," she would cry out. Mom would wander into the beauty parlor attached to the farm home and find Katie with one of her clients, whereupon Mom would offer advice on how she should be styling the client's hair.

More than once, Mom walked in on Katie as she held a conference with the women who work for the Private Duty Companion Care business my sister owns and manages from the farm. Everyone was sitting around the big dining room table when Mom entered, "Oh," she said with a big smile, "Are we having a party?" Then sat down and acted as if she was a welcome visitor to a Tupperware party. Life is quirky and peculiar when you share breathing space with an Alzheimer's victim.

After a long summer of Mom in Katie's personal space, Sis advises me to keep our door locked and maintain as much privacy as possible. "Your sanity depends on it," she warns. Mom makes her way to our front door several times a day. It frustrates me but I instantly feel guilty about not wanting to tend to her; after all, it's why I'm here, why I've *chosen* to be here.

Knock-Knock-Knock-Knock-Knock-Knock

I paste a smile on my face and answer the door, "Hi Mom, how ya do'n?"

"Do you have any toothpicks?" She asks in the same anxious tone someone would ask for a tourniquet while bleeding to death.

"Yes, I have toothpicks, but so do you at your house."

"I do!" She is absolutely amazed she has toothpicks. "Where are they?"

"They're in the drawer below your microwave."

She thinks for a few seconds with a cloud of doubt in her eyes and then warily says, "Oh, Ok." She turns to leave but just before shutting the door, she peeks back in and asks, "What's a microwave?"

When she asks questions like that or "What's fruit?" the wind blows out of me as if I've been sucker-punched. I gasp, take a deep breath and walk her back to her house. I open the drawer below the microwave and find seven packages of the little plastic toothpicks my parents like to use. *Seven*!

"Oh, look at that, we do have toothpicks!" She acts as if we just discovered a drawer full of lollypops.

"Yes, you certainly do have toothpicks and, look, you even have a microwave." Shame on me for saying this since she's just admitted she doesn't know what a microwave is.

She looks at me in complete disgust, "Well, how the hell am I going to clean my teeth with a microwave?"

I deserved that, don't you think?

# 8

# "Cookies? We Have Cookies!"

Trying to keep Mom busy and occupied is a great challenge. She's never been interested in watching television but she will sit and watch a movie with me if I can find something without profanity. This strikes me as highly ironic, since she can be the queen of profanity even on her best days. We watch *Cinderella* or *Ann of Green Gables*, *Cinderella* or *Ann of Green Gables*, *Cinderella or...* I have both movies memorized. Even with her hearing aids, she can't hear very well, so we use subtitles: "Put those words at the bottom of the T.V. for me," she instructs, "they make me believe what I heard is what I heard."

She loves a bird book I have; each page has a picture and several paragraphs of information about the bird, along with a button you push to hear the bird sing. She is pleased as punch when we sit together for a session of reading and listening. She responds like a child at the various birds. "Mad," she says when we hear a Canada goose. "Sweet soft," she responds at the call of a Black-Capped Chickadee. "Noisy!" she remarks at the sound of the raven. This past summer, Katie noticed Mom using these one-word responses, like a child first learning to talk. It was a clue she had experienced what our family calls another "nose dive." My mother has become my little girl.

Last winter she was my sassy, angry teenager. Her outbursts frustrated me to tears almost every day just as I'm sure my teen years did the same for her. Alzheimer's makes us play a hellish game of "Tit for Tat."

Katie and Del had to rescue us last winter when Mom sapped our energy and emotional strength. We haven't needed a rescue party this winter. Mom's teen years are over, now she's a toddler. Through careful consultation with Mom's doctor, we have finally found a combination of prescriptions that ease her anxiety without turning her into a zombie. We take her to her favorite restaurants and for slow walks around the mobile home court. We do anything to keep her content. I admit I'm getting tired of the bird book activity. "Read birds," she asks one day. I can't help but groan and then remember my favorite childhood book. She must have read *The Little Engine That Could* hundreds of times to me. I owe her for all she did for me but I need a new activity. "Mom, let's make cookies." "Cookies!" she responds, just like a three year old.

She toddles behind me like a lost puppy, but as soon as we get in the kitchen, a part of her brain kicks in and she questions me in a monotone yet "Mother knows best" voice, "Is the butter at room temperature?"

I take a deep breath, "Yup, the butter is at room temperature."

I really do try to answer patiently; I should have angel wings the size of elephant ears for my efforts. After asking how to unwrap the butter, she looks at me with the cloud of Alzheimer's suddenly gone from her eyes, "Did you remember to preheat the oven?" For a second I think she's back and the last few years have been a big nightmare. But no, her next question is, "What are we making?"

What is it like to have a brain that remembers the old but not the new? How do you keep the pieces of your life connected?

Here's the rub—Mom was a baker. Not only in our farm kitchen did she whip up her magic, but also in the bakery at the local IGA in Sandusky, Michigan. I often stopped by for short chats with her on the way home from my shift as a nurse's aide at McKenzie Memorial Hospital. It was entertaining to watch her make piecrusts. She worked like a machine and loved every minute of the tedious, repetitive details:

Tear off a handful of dough from the huge mound.
Toss it on the scale.
Pinch off a piece...or
add a smidgen.
Expertly roll the dough in a perfect circle.

Holding the dough as if bathing a newborn baby, she would fold the circle of dough in half, gently place it in the pie tin and unfold it as if it were a rose petal. She quickly patted the dough into the pie tin, deftly crimped the edges with her fingers and thumbs, placed the finished crust off to the side and grabbed a fistful of dough to repeat the whole process.

It was mesmerizing to watch, hypnotic even. I'm sure

she herself would get lost in the act. It's hard to believe, but it's true: She could make 60 piecrusts in an hour. Yes, sixty. One a minute. Now she can't remember for 30 seconds that we are making cookies.

Today she expertly whacked two eggs together, neatly opened them, and knew how to turn on her old Hobart industrial mixer. She can't tell you her zip code, she doesn't know her phone number, and she struggles to give the hospice nurse her full name. However, she can remember how to get the large beater off the mixer. When I struggle with it, she impatiently shoves me to the side, "Here, let me do it," and without hesitation removes the beater.

It's just a laugh a minute, this Alzheimer's.

Mom has always been at home with a 50-pound sack of flour. We would walk home from school and the smell of yeast met us at the driveway. Bread was her specialty. Potato bread, she called it. She boiled potatoes, saved the water, mashed the potatoes and added both water and potatoes to the yeast and flour. She would put the dough in the car and drive around to visit Lee or Waneta, her favorite "coffee klatch" friends. The dough would rise in the car as the coffee perked and the conversations got lively. In between stories and coffee, she would punch down the dough, let it rise again, visit some more, then drive home to roll it out and braid the bread in beautiful long loafs.

Today she can't comb her own hair.

I always loved how the car smelled like yeast. Once I had my license, I always knew to look in the back seat before taking off with the car. There could be a large bowl of plump dough working itself into a puff, even if Mom didn't go visit'n, the car was always her favorite place to raise dough. To this day, warm bread slathered with butter is my ultimate comfort food.

So, here we are in the kitchen together, years later, and she needs help dropping the cookies by the spoonful onto cookie sheets. The same cookie sheets we used back in the 60's when we churned out cookies as if we were Keebler Elves. Under Mom's direction, Sis and I made pounds of cookies and sent them to soldiers in Vietnam along with letters of cheer.

Mom asks for the scoop she once had, a scoop that made perfectly round cookies. She looks for it in the drawer but it's been long gone from her kitchen supplies. When the cookies come out of the oven, she asks like a child if she can have one. She sits at the table crunching away. Five minutes later, she can't remember that she ate a cookie, but she's still looking for the cookie scoop she had 30 years ago. "I'll look for it, Mom, you go have another cookie."

"Cookie?" she asks, "We have cookies?"

If I get this disease I hope someone will read, *The Little Engine That Could*, make cookies with me, and hold my hand as they lead me on slow walks. Whoever that person is, I promise to help them grow a pair of angel wings.

The cookies Mom and I made were Dad's favorite. He called them—

## Scutterbotch Drops

1 cup flour
1 teaspoon baking soda
½ teaspoon salt
1 and 1/2 teaspoons cinnamon
¼ teaspoon ground nutmeg
1 cup butter
(*softened to room temperature as Mom would direct*)
½ cup firmly packed brown sugar
(*more or less, Dad didn't like sweet cookies*)
2 eggs
1 teaspoon vanilla flavoring
3 cups old fashioned oats
½ package butterscotch flavored chips
1 cup coarsely chopped walnuts
(*or more, Dad liked nuts*)
1 cup raisins or dried cranberries
½ cup shredded coconut
¼ cup molasses plus 1 tablespoon water

Preheat oven to 375 degrees

Get the raisins soaking in the molasses. You can put the mixture in the microwave just until the liquid starts to bubble.

Combine flour, baking soda, salt, cinnamon, and nutmeg in a bowl and set aside.

Combine butter, (*Did you remember to soften the*

*butter?*) sugar, eggs, vanilla flavoring. Beat until creamy then gradually add flour mixture.

Stir in the rest of the ingredients. Drop cookies by tablespoon onto ungreased cookie sheets, then push down a bit with the back of the spoon.

Bake in preheated oven (*You did remember to preheat, right?*) for 7 - 12 minutes depending on how big your cookies and how temperamental your oven. Also depends if you want them soft or crunchy or if you want the cookies NOW!

Have fun with your cookies, Mom and I did.

# Mom's Potato Bread

8 oz cake yeast
2 cups warm water mix together
2 teaspoon sugar

4 teaspoons salt
½ cup sugar              mix together and add
½ butter

6 eggs
2 cups warm milk
4 or 5 cooked potatoes mix together
2 cups of saved warm potato water

Add 6 cups flour and mix well.
Now add yeast mixture and mix well.
Add 16-18 cups of flour kneading in 6 cups at a time.
Place in a large greased bowl.
*Put it in the back seat of the car and go have coffee with your girlfriends.*
Let rise until doubled then punch down.
Divide dough into 8 portions.
Mom rolled each dough portion flat, cut into thirds, braided the dough, put into greased bread pan, and let rise.
Bake at 375 degree preheated oven for 30 minutes.

# 9

# I Would Rather Burst Into Flames

It has been several years since I have enjoyed the Christmas season. It's become such a consumer's holiday. Ask me even on my best day if I want to go shopping and I will tell you I'd rather burst into flames. I suck in a groan as Dad, once again this year, puts me in charge of finding a Christmas gift for Mom. A year ago, Kate and I cleared their mobile home of a lifetime of accumulations, to the tune of several truckloads. I am reluctant to start filling all the empty spaces with dust collectors (besides, my sister would club me). Alzheimer's victims do better in simple, clutter-free environments. It's a cruel twist of fate that as Mom loses her memory she also loses a lifetime of possessions.

Going through her closet, I decide a new blouse and a pair of slippers is all she needs. Sounds like a simple shopping trip except she hasn't lost the part of her brain that controls her opinion on what she wears. That part is still hanging on strong and it collides with my opinion of what I think looks nice on her. I have learned I can't choose clothing for her; if I do, it just hangs in her closet. Although I feel guilty about taking her with me to shop for her own gift, I also suspect she won't remember the experience come Christmas morning.

We have loud and interesting conversations as we trudge at glacial speed through the department store. Mom has lost one of her hearing aids, so I compensate by raising my voice; everyone gets to hear our banter. I find it very difficult to raise my voice so she can hear without making it sound like I'm shouting in anger. If I slow my speech to try to take away what sounds like anger, she'll snap back with, "Don't talk to me like I'm stupid."

As I hold up a blouse for her to inspect, she wrinkles her nose and states, "It's too loud and busy." I smolder at this comment because, by golly, the shirt she's wearing is an obnoxious red, black and white check, which our family has dubbed "the clown outfit." She has almost lived in it for the last three years.

"Mom, it's not as bad as the one you have on and everyone is tired of seeing you in it." The shoppers near us peek at what she has on and I see a few smirks as they politely turn away. I admit, that wasn't the nicest thing to say but she comes right back with a snappy "OK, when we get home I'll throw it away." We stay at a deadlock on blouses until we find one she likes, one that I know I bought her last year. I'm sure I sent it up to Michigan in the spring. "Well," I think, "She can just have another one." With the blouse trauma over, we head to slippers.

Slippers are easy. She's pleased with several, but now I have to help her choose a pair that's practical and safe. Our neighbors have clued us in on the forays Mom makes into the yard at 3 a.m., so they need to be durable, but they need to look like Greta Garbo would have had them in her closet. Practical, durable, sexy slippers are hard to come by, but we manage to leave the slipper department with a pair that pleases us both.

When we pay for the items, the checkout woman informs us that we can have free gift-wrapping. "Mom, would you like to have these gifts wrapped?" Her eyes light up, she's all for gift-wrapping. Mom has always loved gifts. Her childhood of abject poverty provides her with no happy memories of gift-giving occasions. When she unwraps a gift, she does it very carefully so she can wrap the box back up and set it around the house as a decoration. This is a pre-Alzheimer's idiosyncrasy. She kept a rewrapped gift box for 15 years and, during that time, she moved across country into a much smaller home. It's a serious pathology. Unfortunately, Alzheimer's hasn't ruined this section of her brain yet; she still unwraps gifts slowly and deliberately, as if she's performing brain surgery.

The gift-wrapping department is located at the opposite end of the store, so, like lethargic turtles, we finally make it to the overly joyful wrap lady. She's very patient as Mom slowly comes to a decision about which paper to use for each gift. While I drum my fingers on the counter, she chooses bows as if her life depends on this tiny, insignificant decision. I want to bang my head on the counter. "Clearly," I think, "I'm not the best person to care for an Alzheimer's victim," especially during the Christmas season. A simple shopping trip, which by myself might have taken me 20 minutes, 30 minutes tops, has now moved into its second hour. The wrap lady continues to smile sweetly and I want to rip that saccharine look off her face and ask her if she wants to switch jobs and take my mother home with her.

It seems as if the sun is setting on a completely new day before we make it back to the car and drive home. Mom sits like a zombie and doesn't say a word all the way home. As we pull into the driveway, she looks down at the wrapped packages on her lap and asks, "What's this?"

I am right about her not remembering the shopping excursion. I think of it as a gift from her disease. I would love to take my husband shopping, so I could get just the right gift; he could point it out and then never remember a thing. He returned many gifts over the years until we agreed to delete gift-giving from our life. Hmm. If drug companies could bottle up tiny doses of Alzheimer's, just enough to last a shopping excursion, imagine how short all those post-Christmas return lines would be.

Within 24 hours of our shopping excursion, Mom is at our door with the wrapped gifts asking, "What are these?"

"Those are your Christmas gifts from Dad."

Confusion clouds her eyes: "This past Christmas or the one coming up?"

"The one coming up."

"How long before it's Christmas?"

"Christmas is in three weeks."

She almost loses her balance with this spectacular news. She grabs my arm to steady herself, "I think I almost lost Christmas," she whispers.

Has she not been with me on all the walks we've taken in the last few weeks? We have purposefully strolled past houses decorated to the hilt with plastic and lights. I've done this specifically for her. Our location in central Florida is not in one of the most upscale neighborhoods;

we have nothing but the worst of the worst in decorating schemes. Everyone, it seems, has missed the memo; "More is not more," especially if it's plastic. The ultimate in trash decorating are the inflatable decorations that lie limp during the day. When I drive by deflated bodies of Santa, elves, and reindeer, I think this is exactly what has happened to Mom. Alzheimer's pulls the plug on the inflate button and what is left is just a shell of the person who once was.

On Christmas morning, Mom sounds like a child as she asks, "When can we open presents?"

As she begins brain surgery on the packages, I watch my husband's face. He's horrified by how long it's going to take to open a few packages. He checks his watch, then looks at me, begging with facial expressions to "get the show on the road." After a few boring minutes, Dad finally bursts out in exasperation "Just rip it off!"

When the paper comes off and the lids on the boxes are lifted, Mom is completely surprised and happy with her new blouse and slippers. If I were a lesser person, I could take them from her, wrap them up again, and we could have Christmas all day long with just two gifts.

Hmm. Another gift of Alzheimer's: constant surprise and happiness with just two simple gifts. In my head, I create a little jingle that goes like this:

> Alzheimer's, Alzheimer's
> Bring me some cheer
> Two repeat gifts
> That surprise me all year!

*Photo courtesy of the Katie Frostic collection*

Uncle Herb and his Apple Pie
He not only bakes, he makes jam, plays euchre, fishes Lake
Michigan, plays shuffleboard, and is a woodworker. He's
81 years old, and still picks his own strawberries for his
jam. He's the Patriarch of our family and is dearly loved.

# 10

# Help Is Spelled H-e-r-b

Uncle Herb arrived this winter with two new knees. His old, wishbone legs were splayed enough to allow sheep to pass through. Lon and I are quite happy to have Herb and his new knees with us this winter to help. He was helping his wife die in Michigan last winter; she also had Alzheimer's, so he arrives with a wheelbarrow full of caregiver skills. He's Mom's older brother, the one she tells stories about every time the family gets together. Mom has never forgiven Herb; in a humph, she'll complain, "He never shared his candy."

Mom and her siblings came from a childhood of deprivation. Everything was scarce: food, clothing, beds. Herb and younger brother, Bob, slept on the sofa while Mom and sister Bertie shared a bed in a tiny bedroom. The boys eventually outgrew the sleeping arrangements, which sent Herb pack'n down the block to his aunt and uncle's house. Apparently, they only slept *one* to a sofa in their home.

Up the block and back at the Bloom house: when room became available, one more child arrived to fill the space. My grandparents, Malinda and Gus, were keeping the new arrival a bit of a secret, given the cramped quarters and all. It wasn't until the cat went ahead and had kittens in a box of homemade, flannel diapers, hidden under the bed, did the rest of the family conclude that Uncle Herb's place was soon to be permanently occupied. When baby sister Mary arrived, they put her in a hammock that swung from the ceiling. As soon as he could, Uncle Herb found a bed in the Navy.

Mom never reminisces about Mary in the hammock, but she still loves to tattle on her brother. "Herb shared *bags and bags* of candy with cousin Theresa but he never gave us any," my mom relates as she pushes Bertie on the shoulder, "Ain't that right, Bertie?"

It's the same story every time. Mom tries to convince everyone that Herb was a "brat." It's so stale a story my grandmother would likely say, "That story's so old we need to pack it in a jar with a piece of bread and fresh'n it up." This also was her solution for hard, stale, brown sugar.

Mom continues to tell the story, but in an Alzheimer's fog: she's lost her sense of time. She still thinks that Herb's sleeping down the street, and he's still passing out *"bags and bags"* of candy to Theresa. When I tell her that Herb is taking her to breakfast, she snaps, "I'm not going with him, he's a brat. Tell him to take Theresa."

You see how it's not hard to find something amusing everyday: this Alzheimer's thing can be really entertaining. I've learned to glide quickly over the pain of Mom's forgetfulness and accept the jolly circus it creates.

Herb tolerates Mom's edginess. "Oh, that's just Donna," he laughs. Over the years, he's taken so many pot shots from his sister that the remarks just roll off. We call him our Teflon Uncle.

There are people who know how to help and then there's the rest of the world. Herb has a sixth sense about when and how to step into the confusion of our life and offer assistance. "How about if I come around and take Donna and Gerald to breakfast?" he asks. "I can be there in ten minutes." I cradle the phone to my shoulder as I finish Mom's hair and breathe a sigh of relief, "Perfect timing," I answer. "I just finished getting Mom ready for the day. They'll both be ready when you arrive." Breakfast with Herb is not a half hour-fling. It's an event. It means I get a good two hours to:

Exercise
Do laundry
Pick up some groceries
Vacuum
Clean the bathrooms
Mow the lawn
Weed the garden
Squeeze some fresh orange juice

My two precious hours, no matter what I pack in, are much easier than Herb's two hours. Getting two immobile people in and out of a vehicle is daunting. My parents creak when they walk. They take cautious steps on weak legs, while they hang onto my arm as if we're crossing a rushing river on a narrow plank. The three steps in their home, which they must ascend and descend everyday, have become their own personal Everest. Every movement with them has to be carefully choreographed; I have almost knocked them over simply by opening the car door. Herb wrestles Dad's walker into the trunk and I silently thank Lon who harped at Herb all last summer to get those knees fixed. Just how could this breakfast event get out of the starting gate if he were crippled?

In the five minutes it takes to get creaking people down Everest and over the rushing river, Mom is a snippy chatterbox:

"Do I look good enough to be seen in public?"

"Why aren't you going to breakfast with us?"

"Why am I the only woman in the crowd?"

Herb and I look at each other: we know when Mom says this it's because she misses Herb's wife, Marian. Never close friends as sisters-in-law, they came to find comfort in each other as their shared disease progressed. Alzheimer's provided a way for them to connect and create a sweet relationship that before did not exist.

As I help Mom into the car, I assure her that she'll have a good time, even if she is the only female in the group. While I buckle her seat belt she whimpers, "Why do I always have to sit in the back?" I pat her on the head and tell her she can sit in front next time. I take a deep sigh and blow kisses to everyone as Herb backs out the driveway. He smiles at me as if he's headed to the county fair with a load of teenagers.

He's a jolly soul, the perfect companion for my parents, my personal, caregiver angel. When we invite him to our family dinners, he arrives with freshly squeezed orange juice or a quart of fresh strawberries that he has picked himself. Strawberry pick'n is a lot easier for him this winter, given those new knees and all. On a whim, he'll drop off a bag of Pink Lady apples, which he's carefully chosen from his favorite fruit stand. On December 25, he arrived with two, flowering Christmas cactus, which he found at the flea market that he likes to ramble through: one for Mom and one for me. His best act, one that no one can compete with, is the apple pie with strudel topping that he makes from scratch. When his wife was still with him, he had to hide the pies from her, otherwise she would pick off the top crust of crunchy, cinnamon nubs.

Uncle Herb is patient and kind with Mom, when everyone else wishes she'd disappear. If she is anxious and wants to walk off a storm brewing in her head, Herb holds her hand and they stroll off like lovers. When they return, she's a completely new person. Herb has a magic touch, not only with Mom but also with Dad. Herb calls and announces, "I'll bring the popcorn if Gerald has a movie we can watch." He arrives grinning at the door with a big bag of popcorn, plops on the couch next to Dad, and the two of them spend hours watching Spaghetti Westerns. Dad looks less haggard and has a bit of color to his cheeks just from hang'n with Herb.

My uncle has taught me how to help. "Call me if you need any help," is offered by many well-intending friends and family. I've offered the same gesture to others. But now I know how to help. Now I know you offer something specific:

"Is Donna ready to go out for breakfast?"

"Here's a bag of apples."

"I baked this pie just for you."

I've learned you should arrive with a flowering, magenta cactus and announce, "Have you ever seen so many blooms on one cactus!"

Uncle Herb's been a great teacher; now I'm ready to offer the kind of help someone really needs. I can't wait to boldly arrive at someone's doorstep with toilet brush in hand and proclaim, "Hi! I'm here to clean your bathroom."

It's so much more suitable than "Call me if you need help."

Don't you agree?

# Uncle Herb's Apple Pie
*Herb's instructions in Italics*

## Crust

2 cups flour      1 teaspoon salt 1/2 cup olive oil
( *"...extra virgin, if you can get it."*)
4 1/2 tablespoons cold water
(*"...you have to put ice cubes in the water to make it real cold, do that ahead of time"*)
Mix just enough to hold the ingredients together, and then roll out using extra flour to keep it from sticking. Pat the dough into a 9 to 10 inch *deep* dish pie pan. Trim excess dough along the edges.

## Filling

8 medium apples (Herb uses McIntosh or Gala)
1/2 cup sugar 1 teaspoon cinnamon
3 Tablespoons corn starch
(*".... It helps thicken the pie so it's not runny"*)
Peel, core and slice the apples
Mix everything together with a spoon until apples are well coated. Put apple mixture into the pie pan.

<u>Topping</u>

1/2 cup sugar 3/4 cup flour
1/4 cup butter or margarine
*("…. Don't take the butter out of the fridge until you're ready to mix it with the flour and sugar")*
*"Mix it all together with a pastry blender just until it's nice and crumbly, don't mix it too long because the butter starts to get too soft."*

Spoon the topping over the apples.
Bake at 400 ° for 40-50 min.

*Photo courtesy of the Gwen O'Leary collection*

Mom in the apron I sewed for her to wear as an eating apron. The first time I put it on her, she whisked it off and snipped "Bibs are for babies!" "I agree," I assured her "Bibs are for babies, but aprons are for ladies and you're a lady." She wore her apron for every meal, often smoothing it across her lap and adjusting it as if she were a little girl in a crisp new party dress.

# 11

# When Life Hands You Alzheimer's, Make Aprons!

To cope with the endless duties of care-giving, I spend off-duty time in my sewing room. I'm self-medicating with fabric. In two months, I've churned out 22 aprons. With the remnant fabric, I've made two dozen baby bibs, five drawstring bags, and two tubes used to store plastic bags. My bedroom has a face-lift with decorator pillows on the bed, and new designer curtains grace the windows.

You'd think I didn't have a full-time job as a caregiver. I'm excited about my sewing time and the escape it gives me. Remember when I said that I intended to sit by Mom's deathbed and coax her out of this world? Well, she's having none of that. She has never slept in her new bed and I have a feeling we may be down here again next winter, wearing caregiver caps again.

Turns out Mom loves my sewing room and tries to wiggle her way into my private time. Since my purpose for being here is to take care of her, I begrudge her some sewing activities. I've discovered she's quite good at helping with some tasks. She can cut out bibs, turn them right-side out after I've sewn them, and weave strings through casings on drawstring bags. I watch in amazement as she turns under ¼-inch of fabric, without the aid of a ruler, along a 36-inch strip of fabric; she irons it smooth as she nimbly rolls the fabric with her fingers. I measure her work when she's done, all along the strip the turned fabric is precisely ¼-inch. Apron ties become Mom's specialty in my sewing room; it's no wonder I can crank out so many. Lon tells me that I've created an Alzheimer's sweatshop.

Mom sits quietly next to me and gets absorbed in the task; it calms her and makes her feel useful. The first time I had her turn bibs to right-side out, she worked for about a half hour without a struggle. I was surprised that she could complete the task as they can be quite tedious. It wasn't long though before she snipped at me, "If you're going to make me do this every time I come over, I'm not coming over any more." Lon heard her comment and yelled from the living room, "Get that in writing!" It doesn't help to remind her that she was the one who came over and begged to help. Reasoning with an Alzheimer's victim is as successful as reasoning with a colicky baby.

Mom is amazed with what I've created in my sewing room. She turned to my husband after admiring my latest apron and said, "She's really a talented lady. Did you know that?"

"I know" he answered "she's my wife, that's why I married her."

"Well," she retorted. "Don't take all the credit, I was the one who raised her."

Conversations with Mom usually go along this same

vein, but, truth be told, conversations with her have always been a bit frayed around the edges. With Alzheimer's it's easier to turn the other cheek at her barbed comments.

I've learned to sew with her standing over my shoulder. Her head is near mine as she watches intently, as if I am about to launch a rocket. This takes such incredible patience on my part; my zone of personal space is quite narrow, more so than most people I know. Besides, Mom and I have never been bosom buddies. One day, while watching she commented, "You're so smart. How do you know how to do this?"

I turn and look at her in surprise: "Mom, you were the one who taught me how to sew."

She steps back; her eyes are wide with shock. The look on her face is the same look that I would have if someone told me I taught Michelangelo how to paint the Sistine Chapel.

"I did not," she tells me, then follows with, "Don't lie."

I want to hug her and say, "It's the truth." I wish she could remember, as vividly as I can, the many hours she spent teaching Sis and me all the nuances of fabric, specific stitches, and how to read a pattern. She prodded me to become the seamstress I am today. Her voice rings in my ears every time I make a mistake and need to rip out a seam: "A good ripper, makes a good sewer." She taught Sis and me all she knew about sewing. I was a stubborn student; the tedious task of sewing tiny, even stitches in a hem came hard to a tomboy who wanted to romp in the hay barn with my brothers.

While working on the hand sewn hems of our skirts for a 4-H Project, Katie pointed out how easy it was to hem her striped, pastel skirt. "See how the stripes repeat themselves? It's a nice guide to follow, so I can sew consistent stitches." The fabric for my skirt was large, pink, cabbage roses; no repeat pattern provided a guide as I struggled to make my stitches neat and concise. "Can you think of a way I can make mine as easy to hem as Katie's?" I asked Mom. "Yes, I think I know a way," she responded. For a moment I thought the tedium would end. Mom would come to the rescue with a magic trick; there was hope. And then my heart fell, "You're just going to have to stick to it and get the job done." Mom was more patient than I was stubborn and my stitches finally did make their way around the heavily-gathered skirt—neat and concise enough to win a blue ribbon at the county fair. That old blue ribbon is 46-years-old, but I remember the hem of that skirt so vividly that it still makes me shudder. I don't know if I should weep or laugh at Mom's inability to recall the guidance that she gave us.

This is the crazy thing about Alzheimer's; she *can* remember parts of her past but not others. I'm also discovering that she remembers things that fall in the short-term category. She remembers every day that I have a sewing machine and that I've been sewing. She knocks on my door and asks, "Is there any sewing to do?" Every night she is shocked that she has pajamas; the same 'ol jammies continue to surprise her at bedtime. It's another gift of Alzheimer's; you constantly see things as fresh and new. How nice would it be to have different pajamas every night?

I wonder if I will get this disease that delivers new pajamas at bedtime. I worry that Lon is going to get stuck caring for me when my Alzheimer's rears its ugly head. I don't let the worry ruin my day, but I am making a list of accomplishments, which I want him to tell me when I get as far gone as Mom. Here's my list:

- I created a system of food distribution that cured world hunger.
- I met with the Palestinians and the Jews and through my persuasion, they no longer fight.
- I created a Department of Peace to replace the Department of War.
- Brad Pitt was secretly in love with me.
- I sang with *Peter, Paul and Mary.*
- I wrote a best selling novel.

When someone mentions Mom's past accomplishments, she sits with a strange smile; wrinkles of confusion map her face. It is heartbreaking that she can't remember her fine talents. She was known for the wonderful quilts that she gave at baby and wedding showers. Her painted ceramics still decorate her home; one of her oil paintings is in her living room. Her crocheted afghans are tucked away in her hope chest. She taught Bible school, Sunday school, sang in the church choir and loved her duty as camp counselor. On the farm, she could drive a tractor pulling a six-bladed plow through a field as deftly as she could sew a straight seam. Dad taught her how to weld, and together with my two brothers, the four of them had a side business that helped pay the mortgage on the farm.

She worked like a man, my mom. I believe that she loved such work more than the traditional household "women's work." She taught my sister and me how to do all the household work while she managed our farm. She told me once that one of her favorite memories was to come in from the fields to find the house clean, the boys doing their chores while Sis and I got dinner on the table, often with a baby on our hip. Sis and I took in babysitting for our spending money; under Mom's direction, we learned baby-sitting skills and were capable at 11 and 12 to mind a six-month-old and four-year-old.

It is frustrating for her to feel so useless. She was such a busy, talented, woman who never sat still. Alzheimer's has robbed her of her gardening, baking, painting, knitting, and ceramics. I'm lucky to have stumbled on an activity we both enjoy. She's at home with fabric and still has an eye for matching colors and prints. I take her to Wal-Mart, put her in a wheel chair, and head to the sewing department with a few swaths of prints from my stash of fabric. From the wheel chair, she can point to fabric that coordinates with the pieces we've brought. Her eye for finding the right hue or print has not been damaged; she is spot on and offers great advice. Here's the crazy part, the next day she will dress herself with stripes, prints, and colors that make her look like she's headed to a Halloween party as a homeless bag lady.

Our hours together have provided me the time to sew aprons for several of my friends. They are a gift from me, my mom, and Alzheimer's. Without Alzheimer's, I wouldn't be here taking the time to be with Mom, nor would I have sought an activity that serves us both so well. We sit side by side, not saying much, enjoying the feel of fabric and seeing the fruits of our labor in simple little items we stitch together. We both find a calm, peaceful place as we self medicate with fabric.

# 12

# Are You Looking For Sympathy?

I love Phyllis, the home health aide from hospice, who arrives twice a week to give Mom a shower. Phyllis is tiny, spry, and strong as a horse. She can wrap Mom around her little finger and get the job done before Mom has time to stamp her foot and complain, "Now, what's going on here?" Mom stopped taking regular showers two-years-ago, so it's a great relief to have Phyllis in our life.

When Mom lost the ability to care for her hygiene, she also stopped washing her clothes and using deodorant. The beard and mustache she acquired gave evidence that she had stopped tending to her facial hair. Her makeup looked as if she worked for Ringling Brothers. Only her hairdo survived; Dad let her drive herself to the beauty shop once a week to get a tightly-teased, stiff hairstyle.

If my Mother understood how she looked and smelled, she would be mortified. Alzheimer's robs her of hygiene skills as surely as it steals her ability to notice food smeared on her clothes and the stale, body odor that's become her signature fragrance. Kate and I tiptoed around the subject of personal hygiene with her, as if she were a hydrogen bomb ready to go off at the sound of running water. Before Alzheimer's joined our family, Mom's personality was not submissive. With Alzheimer's feeding frequently on her brain, she is even less compliant. The task to get Mom clean was not a simple, handholding, "Come on, Sweetie, let's go take a bath," affair. Mom resented and fought the intrusion in her life; it was a tough task to trick her into washing her armpits. Getting her clothes clean was an easier assignment; we whisked them out of her closet, then washed and returned them, using techniques employed by spies in covert operations.

Last winter I managed to get her into the tub or shower every ten days. It required careful cajoling before she would reluctantly resign herself to the bathroom. "Mom, it's been over a week since your last bath, I can smell you. How about a bath today?"

She buried her nose in her armpit, looked at me in disgust and sniped back, "I don't smell a thing."

"Mom, it's time to take a bath."

"If you think I stink, then don't come near me."

"Mom, come on, you can't go out to eat smelling like this. If you take a bath, Dad will take you out to eat."

She didn't buy it. Why should she? He's been taking her out to eat for over a year now in her rumpled clothes and homeless fragrance. She marched up to Dad, put her hand on her hip and demanded, "Gerald, do I smell bad?" He looked at my begging eyes and then back at the wife that he's obeyed for 58 years: "No, I think you smell just fine."

As children, we learned early on that Mom was in

charge. Her body language told us long before her words to stop our horseplay. There was no counting to three in our house. A stamp of her foot, a hand on her hip, and the cloud in those dark, brown eyes were all that was necessary to stop the tom foolery. If she actually had to *tell* us to stop, well, then watch out, the consequences of our actions increased ten-fold. We all learned Mom's silent language and danced carefully around her sly tunes. Dad was her most proficient "dance partner"; he knew when to step back and let her lead.

In my teens, Mom and I constantly battled about my hair. She thought my dark, blonde locks, piled on my head, looked just shy of sluttish. Trying to sneak out of the house one night with my upswept hair, Mom caught me. She looked at Dad and asked, "Gerald, what do you think of your daughter's hair?"

Poor Dad, he missed the cue. He looked up at me, smiled and said, "Looks cute."

I watched Mom's body quickly go rigid and thought, "Dang, now we're both in trouble." To get Dad and me both off the hook, I quickly responded, "All right, I'll change it," and headed upstairs to the bedroom mirror to let my hair down.

Such is the dance we all danced, and here we are 40 years later still trying to waltz without stepping on Mom's toes.

Last winter, every so often, I won the "bath day dance" contest. Mom would storm to the bathroom, slam the door in my face and lock the door. After a few minutes, I slithered down the hall to check for sounds of water splashing. Is she really in the tub or just waiting it out? I actually got on my knees to peek under the door. Sounds pathetic, doesn't it? It was. Mom would hear me and shout out, "Could I have some privacy in my own home!" The next time I 'fox-trotted' her to the bathroom she remembered to throw a towel along the bottom of the door. "No peeking," she demanded. Now how did she remember? The steps in our dance routine get more complicated as Alzheimer's twirls her brain.

This winter, we have Phyllis, along with bathing supplies, nurses, a social worker, and a chaplain. Mom shooed the chaplain off the property, doesn't like the social worker much, tolerates the nurses, but *loves* Phyllis. Mom manages a slight fuss on bathing days. She'll spout at me, "But, what if I don't want a bath?"

"Well, you'll just have to take that up with Phyllis when she arrives."

I've learned the less said, the better. Phyllis knows how to handle Mom and I've learned the best way to use a support team is to...*let them support.* Mom is pliable as putty with Phyllis in charge and does whatever Phyllis asks of her...except get her hair wet.

The usual procedure for Mom's hair is a trip to the beauty salon. Although I mange to recycle her hairdo for several days, I'm tired of the salon trips. I asked Phyllis to wash Mom's hair during her usual shower. Kate and I have been coaxing Mom out of her stiff hairdo. She looks younger in her new, pageboy style and I can easily style her hair at home. How ironic to find myself in charge of Mom's hair after so many years of her trying to be in charge of mine. It's not an enviable assignment.

Several years ago, I met my parents for a weekend of camping in Utah. It was a weekend sans the luxury of showers. My son and I fished, hiked, roasted marshmallows and relaxed. I didn't wash my hair, I wore a ball cap; it was the ultimate, laid back weekend. However, when we said our goodbyes, Mom handed me a $20 dollar bill and said, "Your hair needs some work, go get yourself a perm." I was 39; Mom was still playing hair director.

Hair was always such a production when we were growing up. Mom was barber and stylist for the whole family. My brothers got military buzz cuts, while Kate and I endured stinky home perms. Every Saturday, Kate and I would roll each other's hair, a ritual prelude for Sunday church service. A respectable hairdo was more important than brushing our teeth or having clean fingernails. For years I slept on rollers, the ones that looked and felt like baby porcupines; woe to the female in our house who would consider leaving the house with "bed head."

The first time Phyllis washed Mom's hair, she discovered a side of Mom she had never witnessed. With wet hair, Mom is the devil incarnate. Phyllis came out of the bathroom wide-eyed: "When I was washing your Mom she told me, 'You'd better move your hand out of my ass or I'm going to fart on you. And it would serve you right for getting my hair all wet.' I can't believe your mother talks that way!"

I know some of Mom's anger is due to Alzheimer's, but make no joke about it, when Mom wants to let loose, she can let'er rip. I looked at Phyllis and laughed, "Oh well, that's nothing. When I was a kid and whined about anything, she'd say, 'If you're looking for sympathy, it's in the dictionary between shit and syphilis.' " Phyllis thought the phrase hilarious, "Oh, I can't wait to use it on my son; he's always whining about not having a car."

Mom can still belt me with some verbal whoppers. I think that even without Alzheimer's, she would still order me around. One evening while waiting with Dad at the dialysis clinic, Mom kept pacing and complaining about the wait.

"Mom, we're here to keep Dad company. You're his wife. Why don't you sit next to him and hold his hand?"

She walked up to me, shaking her finger, and from her short, five-foot frame, she stared up at me and barked, "Why don't *you* start watching your sassy mouth!"

Everyone in the room, Dad and I included, had to hide our smirks; I especially, since she probably would have bonked me for laughing if she had seen.

We continue to adjust Mom's prescriptions to help us through her times of agitation, paranoia, and fear. It's a balance to keep her from sparking off with, "Mind your sassy mouth" or on the other hand, talking like a robot. Medicated or not, she's not my mom anymore. Like the layers on an onion, Mom's character and personality have slowly peeled away during the last ten years.

She's not my mother, my mother is gone, and I admit there are days when I detest the woman who has taken her place. I've lost the mother I loved; I'm tending to the needs of a stranger.

Hmmm, seems I'm whining. Maybe I need to go open the dictionary and look for sympathy.

# 13

# Big Girl Panties

I have a few family members who tell me my mother's barbed comments are her normal personality. They say she has always been the party pooper, the one with an arsenal of snide comments. They tell me she is a pro at turning a compliment into a criticism, and brilliant at composing an apology so it sounds like blame. She has zinged me many times with bruising comments. It's great that I can now place the blame on her disease. No one wants a complaining, unappreciative, nagging mommy, least of all me, the worn-out, tired, caregiver daughter.

Our most recent, nagging, health care issue is her new hearing aids. She's stone deaf without them, but a sore in her right ear makes it unbearable for her to wear the aid. We make frequent trips to have it adjusted by Maria, a sweet, Columbian woman, who treats Mom like a princess.

At every visit, Maria greets Mom with a sincere, "Oh

my dear, welcome, come in. Look how beautiful you are today." Maria's words flow like water. Her accent smoothes the edges of our sharp English words; it's as if she sings her sentences.

Mom responds with a deadpan look and replies with a monotone, "You lie."

I hold back a chuckle and think that my Mom should run for a seat in Congress. Maria looks over Mom's head at me with pity filling her eyes; she's taken care of Mom's hearing aid needs for three years and has noticed Mom's brown eyes turn cold and empty.

After Maria takes the hearing aids out to adjust and clean them, she and I can chat openly. Maria will often shake her head and say, "I can tell by her eyes that she is far away from us today."

Mom sits in the chair swinging her feet, then spins the chair in a circle; she's lost in her own little girl world.

Recently on a cold morning, as we made our way to Maria's, Mom complained, "Are you making me miserable on purpose or am I supposed to be enjoying the cold."

"Sorry, Mom, I have your seat warmer on. Is it getting warm?"

"Yes, my ass is warm but the rest of my body is freezing. Turn the heater on," she demands.

I turn and look at her and say in a singsong voice, "Say it nice," just as I instructed my children when they were rude.

"I'll be nice when you make me warm."

I point to the temperature gauge, "Watch this needle: as soon as it moves, we can turn on the heater and warm air will come out. If we turn it on now, we'll just get cold air."

She reaches over, turns the fan on, settles back in her

seat and is quiet for 15 seconds before she barks, "It's cold, turn it off!"

I switch off the fan, take three deep breaths and hold my tongue. I can't reason with her; I can only learn to stay calm and not take her pinpricks personally.

We are both warm and quiet by the time we get to Maria's, but her little shop hasn't opened yet, even though Maria is always prompt. I point to the closed sign on the door, "Looks like Maria's not here yet, so let's just wait in the car where it's warm."

"You drove me all the way over here in the cold so I could sit and wait?"

I try diplomacy: "Let's be kind and just sit here and wait patiently."

"I don't want to wait."

I try diplomacy again: "Mom, my favorite phrase when people whine and complain is *'put your big girl panties on and deal with it.'* If someone says, 'It's too difficult,' I tell them, *'put your big girl panties on.'*"

I keep repeating this phrase with several examples, hoping she gets the message.

Finally, she interrupts and spouts, "If you keep it up, my ass is going to get so big, nobody's panties are going to fit me."

So much for diplomacy, it's as effective as reasoning.

When Maria opens her shop, it's a strain to get Mom out of the car. She is as physically stiff and inflexible as her mind; I worry about breaking a bone as I struggle to get her stubby body out of the car. She walks slowly and deliberately as I guide her into the office where Maria greets us with a trilling, "Good morning. How good to see you. How are you today?"

Mom gives Maria a syrupy smile and stutters a long,

confused, but kind reply. They clutch each other's hands before falling into an embrace.

Maria looks at me across Mom's shoulder and says, "You have such a sweet mommy. You are so lucky."

I weakly smile back and hold back the deep sigh I want to exhale. I would love to tell Maria just how barbed Mom can be, how stubborn and difficult she can be; "sweet" is not an adjective I would use to describe my mother.

But I don't, because, you see, I'm wearing my Big Girl Panties.

# 14

# "How Did You Find Me At That Place?"

Mom's disease has progressed enough for me to trick her into going to an adult day care center. I researched day care centers two years ago when assisting with my Aunt Marian, who suffered from Alzheimer's; I knew back then that we would need day care for Mom, so I scrutinized the few centers available. She now spends four hours a day, two days a week at Dynamic Seniors. I wanted to place her in the center last year but she would have scratched my eyes out and then laid into my Dad for the disgrace of putting her away.

I can't say she loves her day care days as I do, but there's not much fight left in her. "I don't do well in large groups," she tells me, and I reassure her with, "I know, Mom, that's why you go to Dynamic Seniors where there are only eight people."

It's taken me several weeks to muster the courage to

go through with the details of getting her admitted to the center. I don't really need the assistance now, but I know I will. I am researching the options of home hemodialysis for Dad, which will require six weeks of training. I'll need a place where Mom is comfortable while Dad and I learn the process. Kudos to the wise person who said, "Failing to plan is planning to fail." Life has caught me off-guard more than once and I'm all about having safety nets in place. I'm just lazy about getting them primed and ready.

The paper work is daunting. I need a doctor's visit to get documents signed and a TB test, but the real fly in the ointment is how I will actually get Mom to stay at the center when I leave. I imagine her hitting me while I drive her there, crying when I leave, and begging me not to go.

I keep up a nonstop chatter during the ten-minute drive to Dynamic Seniors. I ask questions about her childhood to keep her brain busy and off the topic about our destination. It is very much like taking kids to day care or telling them that they are going to have a babysitter. My four-year-old once responded to the babysitter line with, "Well, Mom, I sure hope she's not blind." Why at four he thought I would hire a blind babysitter is still a puzzle, but those types of responses are similar to Mom's thought processes and comments.

I've given her the prescription advised by her doctor; she's happy enough to believe she's on her way to Cinderella's ball. However, as we pull up to the center, she reads the sign, "Dynamic Seniors Day Care."

Her eyes are wide as she looks at me and asks, "Are you leaving me here?"

I have become very good at using "Alzheimer's Fiblets,":

tiny, nondestructive lies to help Mom continue to feel comfortable in any setting. "You like it here, Mom. This is your social outing. This is what you do every Tuesday and Thursday." I try to make it sound matter-of-fact, as if it's a normal routine. Actually, it's a big, fat lie since she has never been here; it's her first four-hour day and we don't know if she'll like it here.

I give her a quick goodbye as I hand her off to Terry, who cleverly gets Mom distracted as I walk out the door, run to the car, and don't look back. I've armed Terry with Mom's favorite blanket for naptime and three, farm stories I've written with Mom as the main character. She loves the farm stories; it calms her during episodes of agitation.

After four nervous hours on my part, I go back to the center and find Mom sitting at a table, visiting with other seniors. She looks at me with a big smile and greets me, "Hi! It's been a really good day."

When we get in the car she asks, "How far from home are we?"

I let her know that we're only about ten minutes from home. "But none of this looks right, I don't know this area. How did you ever find me back there at *that place*?"

I fiblet, "You've never been on this side of town, that's why it doesn't look familiar."

She's quiet for a few minutes, and then whispers, "I didn't think anyone was going to come and get me and I didn't know how to get home."

I'm flooded with guilt and my stomach does a sickening flip-flop at the confusion she has endured. Did she think during those four hours that we were done with her? Did she really believe she would never see us again? I want to hold her close and promise that I'll never take her back there again, but I know it's important for her to return and get comfortable with the environment. She needs the social interaction and the arts, crafts, and music that Dynamic Seniors offers.

When we pull into the driveway, she's ecstatic. "Oh, it feels so good to be home."

Then, as I walk her through the door, she comments, "It's really hard to be with so many people and not know who is sitting next to you, but now that I'm home I feel a little lonely."

Settled in her favorite chair, she sleeps for the entire afternoon as if a day in the sandbox with friends is too much for her disintegrating brain.

Day care gives us all a break. Dad can have a quiet breakfast with a long, leisurely cup of coffee as he scours the newspaper. Some mornings, Herb, his brother-in-law, picks him up to go out for breakfast. Afterward, they take a relaxing drive through rolling countryside in search of the beautiful cranes that winter in Florida.

With Dad in good hands and Mom at Dynamic Seniors, Lon and I head out to the local gym for our daily workout. Now that Mom's comfortable at daycare the four hours fly by. After the gym, we'll run a quick errand, get home for a shower, grab lunch and it's already time to head out and retrieve Mom.

The retrievals vary only slightly. She's always completely stunned that I have arrived; she's amazed I know how to get to "*this place*" and then, miracle of all miracles, I know how to get home! It makes me laugh, only after it makes me cry.

I workout every day and love the experience of sore muscles—I get sore in places I didn't know I had. I'm also building emotional muscle with my duty as caregiver for dying parents. Every day I feel a new sore spot deep inside; I'm discovering secret passageways in my soul that I never knew existed. It's good to have emotional muscle, without it I would be constantly on my knees for the pain this experience *could* bring. At every twist and turn, I force myself to acknowledge that this is life: intense, raw and beautiful. I have a choice to embrace it and be glad for what it offers or turn and run.

Coming home from day care one day, Mom asked, "Has anyone new arrived?"

Not really knowing what she meant I told her no one had arrived.

Her response was, "But all of the units are ready, right?"

Ah, it hits me: She's back in Steamboat Springs, Colorado, as Head Housekeeper of 76 condominium units. "Yep, all the units are cleaned and ready. I put fresh fruit on the table and stocked the wine."

I often assisted her at the condominiums; I remember all the details involved in getting the units ready. It's fun to add some fine points to my fiblet.

After a moment, she asks, "So, who's at camp?"

I do race laps through my brain, trying to keep up with all the flashes she receives in hers. Now she is remembering all the summers that her four kids went to camp and she herself volunteered as camp counselor.

"No one's at camp. Summer's over and we're all getting ready for school."

She nods, "Oh, that's good."

Reality must be scary for her; we leave her in a strange place and she doesn't know if she'll ever see us again. If living in the past offers comfort, then I'll fiblet my way to hell's gates if that's what gives Mom peace.

When we arrive home and I pull in the driveway, she looks at me with fear and asks, "What's this place?"

It's as if a ton of bricks lands in my lap; I wish I could find a way to fiblet my way out of this one. "This is home, Mom. This is where you live. Dad's inside waiting for you."

Relief floods her face. "Dad's here?" She often refers to my father as "Dad."

She cautiously walks through the door with me, stops to look around, then whispers, "Where's Dad?"

I direct her to the stairs leading to the dining room where he sits waiting. It's an effort for her to pull herself up along the railing. When she sees him she stops and cries out, "Oh, I thought I would never see you again!"

She keeps heading towards him. Her feet are unsteady and she stumbles a bit, but all the while, she continues with a stuttering dialog. "Oh what a beautiful face. Do you know how beautiful your face is? It's like falling in love with you all over again when I see you after so long."

"Wow," I think, "How sweet she can express this, that she actually feels this." If she didn't have this hideous disease, would she be experiencing this incredible love? Without Alzheimer's could she transport herself back to when Dad was the young buck she fell in love with? He's a dying man. He looks frail, old, and tired. Kidney disease has ravaged his body. It's staggering how Alzheimer's clouds her vision. This withered, old man is her young lover. Alzheimer's offers such strange gifts.

Dad greets her with arms out wide. "Well, how are you sweetie?"

They hug and kiss like long-lost lovers as I steady myself at the kitchen counter. It can bring you to your knees, this beautiful life.

I often pause and reflect on how this hideous disease affects our whole family. We have all dug deep to find the strength and energy, both physically and emotionally, to provide support and care. A favorite quote from Susan Straight flashes though my brain: "I've been to sorrow's kitchen and licked clean all the pots." Surely, Alzheimer's is the sorriest kitchen I have ever encountered, but I am willing to lick the pots clean and get Mom through her last journey in life with dignity.

In doing so, I have discovered a sweet surprise, an ironic gift of Alzheimer's. As the disease destroys my mother's character, it builds mine.

# 15

# Hey! I'm Still Me In Here

I think of Alzheimer's as a little Pac-Man scurrying around in Mom's brain, taking nibbles here and there. It's a wild guess as to how long the little Pac-Man has been nibbling. Who can know how long geriatric forgetfulness rode the fence before it hopped over into the Alzheimer's pasture?

This is what I do know—Mom has worked hard to keep her brain intact. Maybe subconsciously she knew she had to keep it oiled with familiar daily tasks. For the past few years, she refused to sit still and spent hours roaming through her Florida yard pulling weeds. Neither she nor Dad could manage the mower anymore, so she kept the yard free of weeds by painstakingly plucking any weed seedling that dared rear its head in her yard.

"Your mother was always working in her yard," the neighbors tell me. "I'm not sure she ever accomplished much, but we always saw her bending over, pulling at something."

In her last years as a gardener, I know it was not about the weeds; it was about keeping busy at a chore that gave her a sense of purpose. She could no longer follow a recipe to cook or bake, so her deep, German, farm roots served her well by keeping her busy at weed pulling. I think of it as a contest: she weeded as diligently as little Pac-Man nibbled. It comforts me that through her diligence she gave Pac-Man a good run for the money.

Now, in the seventy-fifth winter of her life, Mom can no longer pull weeds. She has lost her sense of balance and can no longer bend over, nor can she stay on her legs for more than 15 minutes. She spends many hours in a favorite lounge chair in the corner of her dining room. She begs for something important to do, but stays on task for ten minutes before she asks if she can go sit in her chair.

Today after helping her to the chair and covering her with her favorite blanket, I finished the dishes we had both started as a team. I checked on her one last time before leaving and found her with a pained expression. Deep furrows lined her brow, she pinched her eyes tight and clung to her blanket like a baby.

"Mom, are you ok? Are you in pain? What's wrong?"

She slowly opened her sad, brown eyes and stuttered, "I'm just trying to keep myself glued together. I'm falling apart and I'm just trying to hold onto all of me."

I am stunned and heartbroken as well as amazed and honored that I am here to witness her tenacity. I want to weep in sadness and cry for joy.

"My gosh, what a fight you have in you," I think.

I give her a hug but cannot come up with any words to communicate back to her. Isn't it amazing that the brain with Alzheimer's has managed to communicate so clearly to me and I'm the one who's at a loss for words?

Mom delights me with the way she communicates her feelings. She jumbles her words, but she is spot on about the meaning. Our family dislikes the dialysis clinic in Florida where Dad spends four to five hours, three times a week. The office clerk at the front desk has the personality of Nurse Ratched from *One Flew Over The Cuckoo's Nest*. She has tested my patience more than once with her rudeness and lack of empathy. When gathering up Dad at one in the morning, I often find wastebaskets sitting on empty dialysis chairs. When I question this unsanitary practice, they want me to believe that it's best for the cleaning people and does not pose a problem. I don't even want to know the excuse for the sticky blood on the waiting room chair, which my elbow has rested on. Aside from that, the scheduling is abysmal, and I have nothing else nice to say about the place.

A change in Dad's dialysis session, from afternoon to evening, created challenging times with Mom. Long evening hours without Dad made Mom conclude that he was out to a bar or in jail. Just for the record, my Dad hasn't seen the inside of a bar or held a beer can for about 60 years. He's never been in trouble with the law, let alone spent time in jail. It takes a tremendous effort for Dad to get dressed and walk to the breakfast table, but Mom asks me in all seriousness when he's at dialysis, "Is he out drink'n?"

I break out laughing and think, "Well bless his heart if he is!"

"Do you think this is funny?" she snaps at me. I have to control myself and calmly explain *again* about Dad's dialysis and why he's not home.

We often wait 45 minutes before his dialysis chair is ready. The wait irritates us all, but plays havoc with Mom's demeanor. She paces the floor and asks every few minutes, "What are we waiting for?"

When the nurse comes into the waiting area to get Dad, everyone in the waiting room wants to cheer for joy. One night after helping Dad to his dialysis chair, I had to pull Mom away from the building as she struggled and stuttered, "I don't feel too *confidential* about leaving him in this place."

I wanted to say I didn't feel too *confidential* either, but I just chuckled under my breath. I knew exactly what she meant.

Half way home, she announced, "I don't like that place, I'm not too sure they have all their pegs in the right squares."

Spot on, Mom! I couldn't agree more about those pegs and squares. "I don't really like it either," I tell her, "but Dad can't live without dialysis, so we have no other choice. Dialysis keeps him alive."

Mom wants to know if Katie thinks dialysis keeps him alive, and does my husband think this is what we should be doing. I reassure her that we all agree we have to do this.

She sighs heavily and says, "Well, just so all the important people have the same idea in the same row boat." Her words are a bit twisted, but I get the meaning, don't you?

Listening to victims of Alzheimer's try to get their messages across has provided me with some profound moments. A few years ago, I helped my Uncle Herb care for his wife who suffered from Alzheimer's. He wanted me to take Aunt Marian shopping for some new church dresses. Aunt Marian's Alzheimer's was pretty advanced. I couldn't rely on her staying in a dressing room while I scurried back and forth with dresses for her to try on. It would just be like Marian to march angrily out sans clothing and demand to be taken home. I enlisted my Mom to help with the shopping excursion. Just a few days prior, I had already shopped with Mom, so I knew the routine.

A sales woman had scolded both of us for being in the dressing room together. "Our policy is one person to a changing room!" she snapped.

I took her elbow and walked her away from Mom, "Listen here," I whispered, "my mom has Alzheimer's and I'm sorry about breaking your rules, but I have to help her."

She backed off in fright. Was she afraid of me or did she think that Alzheimer's was a contagious disease?

When I arrived with Mom and Marian, I marched right up to the sales woman and announced, "I know you only allow one person in the dressing room, but I'm here with my Aunt who has advanced Alzheimer's. My mom's Alzheimer's is not quite as bad, so she's going to help my aunt in the dressing room."

I wanted to sit and sob from the look of sorrow the saleslady gave me. I'm a much tougher broad if people are rude and nasty to me; pity makes me weep.

I left Mom to help Marian try on some new bras while I hunted for dresses. I raced back to the room with several dresses only to find Mom and Marian almost in tears. "She doesn't know how to get her bra on," Mom yelled at me.

Sure enough, there stood Marian all confused with the bra strapped above her ample bosom.

"Marian, bend over and shake your boobies into the bra," Mom demanded.

With both Mom and I pulling, tugging, and trying one dress after another, we dressed and undressed Marian several times. All the while, she asked to go home and complained, "Why is it so cold in here?"

At one point, I draped several dresses on her to keep her warm while I rushed out to find something that would fit her. "Don't let her get dressed," I ordered Mom.

At the end of 90 minutes, we all wanted to cry and go home.

In the end, we found two dresses and two bras and Marian was delighted with them all. As I helped her out of the final dress, she started to cry, "But I like this one. I want to keep it on. Don't I get to keep it?"

Mom snapped, "You can't wear this out of the store. We have to pay for it."

I leaned against the wall of the dressing room and closed my eyes thinking, "Mom's being a brat, Marian is a four-year-old and I'm in charge." This is not how I thought I would spend my retirement.

By the time we arrived to show Uncle Herb the purchases, we were all giddy and happy about the shopping adventure. Mom was excited to tell her brother about the dresses, while I tried to relay what a circus it was to shop with both of them. Marian stood next to us, anxiously standing on one foot then the other, and finally managed to get our attention. She stopped several times and stuttered, but managed to say, "I just want you all to know...um that, um, no matter what it looks like on the outside...I, I, I'm still *me* in here. I'm still the...same, same person I've always been."

We all stood in shocked silence. I wanted to sink

into the floor and thought that I should have been more patient. Maybe I had dressed and undressed her without regard to her confused feelings. Maybe I had treated her too much like a big rag doll, and I should have been gentler. I hugged Marian. We all did, and we assured her that we knew she was still with us, that she was still the same person she always was, and that she was "still in there."

I went home and wrote down exactly what she said. I remember thinking, as she stuttered and managed to get her few sentences out, that it was a very profound moment, a privileged moment I would never forget. Assisting with Marian's care was my training ground. I don't regret my decision to be here with Mom as she fights to "hang onto herself." Someday, I too may have to squeeze tight to keep myself glued together.

If that's what my future holds, I hope the important people making decisions for me are sitting in the same rowboat.

*Photo courtesy of the Katie Frostic collection*

My mom and her mother—Malinda Bloom
When Grandma flew west to visit me in Colorado, she unpacked a roast from her suitcase when she arrived. She assured me it was frozen when she packed it and completely safe to eat—this from a woman who fed me roadkill.

# 16

# Grandma Fed Us Roadkill

It's a beautiful, spring morning in Florida as I guide Mom to the car. We are on our way to Dynamic Seniors Day Care. I point out the cardinal singing on the power line across the street. Her sight is excellent; she spots the bird immediately. But her ears gave up long ago. Hearing aids are a poor substitute and she doesn't hear the beautiful melody. We stop and stay in one spot like statues. "Listen carefully, Mom. It's a beautiful song."

I watch her strained face as she struggles to hear and suddenly the light goes on in her eyes. "Oh, I *can* hear it," she says in surprise.

Our resident mockingbird adds his song to the morning chorus. He sounds like an old, squeaking screen door. I point out the mockingbird to Mom. "See how his tail is fan-shaped."

"He doesn't sound too good," she tells me.

I'm surprised she has heard his raucous cry. "He's

imitating a rusty hinge," I tell her. "Sheena has a mockingbird that sounds just like her telephone ringing." Sheena's our friend from Scotland, who visits twice a year. An annoying mockingbird in her yard kept her running in to answer the phone. He would "sing his ring" just as she sat to have a drink on her patio.

Mom laughs at the story and says, "But Archie can't ever come to Florida again, can he?"

She continues to astound me with what she can and can't remember. She knows that Sheena's husband, Archie, can't travel to the States because of his health. She never remembers that Dad has renal failure and spends three days a week in dialysis.

Our driveway chatter has not just been about bird-watching and talking about friends: I have her favorite blanket in the dryer and I'm stalling for time. It's my new trick, if I keep her temperature at a comfortable level, her *temperament* follows. I guide her into the car then make a quick dash back inside for the warmed blanket. I tuck it under her chin, along her legs and under her feet.

"Oh, that feels so nice, it makes me want to get out every morning," she stutters. "I could ride forever under this coziness."

We are only a few miles from home when her eyes glaze over and she looks like she's in heat stroke under the blanket. It's 70 degrees Fahrenheit, the sun is shining, the blanket is a little overkill, but I've spent too many mornings listening to her carp about how cold it is. If I put myself in her reality, life moves along smoothly. My personal coaches, the social workers from hospice, have instructed me on techniques to help Mom feel comfortable in her various stages of reality. They wisely advise, "You have to understand that for her, whatever she is thinking or saying, it is her sense of reality, no matter how disconnected it may seem to you."

When she asks me, "Did you feed the ducks?" I answer, "Yep, the ducks are fed." We haven't had ducks since I was ten, but if she thinks we have ducks, then by golly, we have ducks. If she says she's cold, we throw blankets on her, no matter what the thermometer reads.

As we pass the cemetery, I notice the car ahead of me swerve and hit a black cat running across the road. It looks intentional. I hear Mom ask, "Did that car just run over the cat on purpose?"

I was hoping she hadn't noticed the sickening scene. As we drive past, I look into the rearview mirror, Mom sees me and asks, "Is it dead?"

I hate to tell her the truth; the cat is writhing on the road. I'm tempted to turn back and put it out of it's misery, but it's an act I don't want to do with Mom in the car. I hold my breath and hope she doesn't ask me to go back.

She just might, her mother was known for her roadkill cuisine.

When eating at his mother-in-law's, Dad always cautiously asked, "What's the meat in the stew?"

It could be muskrat, sheep, or rabbit. Recently, Kate related a time when we were on the road with our Grandma Bloom: "I saw Grandma step on the gas and swerve to hit a jackrabbit. Then she stopped the car, got out the tire iron and finished off the rabbit. I remember her happy 'Whoop' of delight before she threw it in the trunk."

My jaw drops; I ask, "What did she do with it?"

"She skinned it and cooked it up for us to eat."

"Grandma fed us roadkill? I don't remember that. How old were we?"

"I was around eight, you must have been seven."

"Did I eat any?"

"I don't know if you did," she answers with a smirk on her face, "but I know I didn't."

We both crack up laughing about the incident, I mockingly scold, "Thanks for watching out for me!"

Mom leans forward and tries to see the cat through her side mirror. I hold my breath, thinking she's going to ask me to go back and pick dinner off the road. This is one instance where I'm not going to put myself in her reality. I am resolved about this: I am not cooking cat for dinner.

Mom just sits back and shakes her head. I wonder if she still remembers much about her mother. I carefully construct a statement, a technique the social worker's have taught me. Instead of asking a "remember" question, I make a statement in the direction I want her to go and see if she can follow the conversation.

"Mom, I had a conversation with Bertie about Grandma Bloom selling fruits and vegetables from the trunk of her car."

The memories are still with her, and she's able to tell me about the fresh eggs that Grandma gathered along with fruits and vegetables from her garden. She drove to Saginaw and sold her wares to her regular customers. "She would butcher a chicken or a rabbit and get the meat seasoned and dusted with flour, ready for her customers to put in the frying pan," Mom proudly chatters about Grandma's resourcefulness all the way to Dynamic Seniors.

After I drop her off, I begin to wonder. "Did Grandma ever sell *roadkill* from her trunk?" The thought makes me smile, I make a mental note to share this thought with Katie.

She's going to love it!

## Rabbit Stew
A recipe Grandma would have loved

1 three pound rabbit
6 small onions, chopped
1 bay leaf
½ cup chopped celery
2 tsp. salt
2 cups diced carrots
3 raw potatoes, cut up
3 tbs. flour
1 tbs. chopped parsley

Clean rabbit and soak in salted water. Drain, disjoint it in pieces for serving and place in a large kettle with onions, bay leaf, celery and salt. Cover with cold water and cook slowly until tender, about two hours. Add chopped carrots and potatoes and continue cooking until these vegetables are done. Smooth flour with a little cold water and add slowly. When thickened, add chopped parsley and serve.

*Recipe credit: http://www.bowhunting.net/susieq/rabbit.html*

# 17

# Music In My Toes

Age has made me shameless. The older I get the more willing I am to toot my own horn. I admire what I create with fabric, paper, soil—even words. I turn junk into interesting pieces of yard art or functional furniture for the house. Alas, my many talents do not extend into the world of music. My secret wish has always been to sing and play a stringed instrument.

Katie and I started piano lessons around the age of ten; I knew right away that it was not my gig. I didn't enjoy studying classical music. The notes, rhythm, and precision were too exacting for my patience. I hated the rigidity of practice, recitals intimidated me and I thought my instructors were a bore. My sister loved it. While her fingers sashayed over the ivory, mine hunted and pecked for the correct keys. Could it have been all the practice she put in everyday? Kate was dedicated; she set a timer to make sure she didn't short herself a complete hour of practice. I didn't view it as *practice* so much as the ultimate in brown-nosing. I woke up every day hoping to weasel my way out of all those long, laborious practice sessions.

I was as stubborn as Mom was insistent. She'd ask, "Why can't you sit and practice like Katie?"

You can imagine how much I liked that form of encouragement. It did not endear me to my mom, my sister, or the piano. Hate it or not, I was stuck with lessons for seven years. After 40 years of not playing, I'm lucky to find middle C; I struggle to stomp out a decent rendition of chopsticks.

Mom's childhood was miserable. At a family reunion, we gathered all the siblings together and asked them to relay one of their happiest childhood memories. Herb, Bertie, Mom and Mary all looked at us dumbfounded, then sheepishly shrugged their shoulders. Apologetically, they mumbled, "We don't have happy memories."

I now realize piano lessons allowed Mom to live vicariously through us. Given the small budget she had to work with, Mom was heroic in her efforts to give us the childhood she never had. She squeezed pennies tight enough to buy a piano and every week we had an envelope with money to pay our instructor.

Piano lessons were the tip of the iceberg. Mom unleashed her talents to decorate our humble farm home; she sewed matching bedspreads and curtains for all the bedrooms, made drapes for the living room, and reupholstered furniture. In December, she decorated a Christmas tree for our bedroom with pink balls, pink ribbons, and pink lights. It was as if Pepto-Bismol met "O, Christmas Tree." She transformed swaths of dotted, Swiss fabric into crisp, new dresses for Easter. On Sundays, Kate and I marched into Sunday school carrying beautiful white Bibles with pages as thin as tissue paper and Jesus' words in red.

When our birthdays arrived, Mom armed herself with Wilton's cake decorating implements and bags of frosting. She swirled pink roses on a little pedestal and carefully arranged dozens of them around the cake. Ribbons of green became leaves, and birthday greetings and names were painstakingly squeezed out of the frosting tubes.

Sis and I knew any gift-giving occasion would bring a new charm for our bracelets that were the rage back in the 60's. We had surprise "Sweet Sixteen" birthday parties, bonfires in the backyard, marshmallows and s'mores, and boxes of sparklers for 4th of July celebrations. We spent weeks camping along the shores of Lake Huron where campfires and weenie roasts, ghost stories, and "Kumbaya My Lord," were pre-bedtime rituals. Norman Rockwell would have admired the childhood that my mother painted for her children.

When eighth grade graduation came around, first for Kate and then me, we walked proudly down the aisle in knee-length, organdy and chiffon dresses. Recently, I learned about the dubious acquisition of those gorgeous dresses. My dad's baby sister Maureen, eight years older than Katie, no longer lived at home, but her closet still held her beautiful clothes. Mom decided the dresses were free game and boldly marched into her mother-in-law's house to choose two perfect dresses for us. Grandma didn't stop her and Kate and I ended up with great dresses. Poor Aunt Maureen felt violated—and rightly so!

My cousins played the accordion and I loved the upbeat swing of "Beer Barrel Polka." They squeezed out lively Polish dance tunes while I plunked out Bach, Beethoven, and Mozart, suitable for funerals. After many months of begging, Mom finally relented and allowed me to take accordion lessons.

While happily practicing one night, my brother Gordon came and said, "Mom told me to tell you that if you can't play *real* accordion music then you should quit playing, it sounds terrible." My relationship with the accordion was short-lived.

I will admit that Kate and I did have fun playing piano every morning at Black River, the one room, country schoolhouse we attended. "The Battle Hymn of the Republic," "Star Spangled Banner," and "America the Beautiful," came every day after the Pledge of Allegiance. We took turns on the old upright piano as the rest of the school stood patriotically and sang. At church, we played hymns for services and special music events. Our forte was playing duets together as we sat side by side, counting softly to keep in time, as twenty fingers learned to sound like one pair of talented hands. We were a hit at family parties, especially at Grandma O'Leary's home where we performed on her impressive grand piano.

Although Mom never begged us to play any favorite tunes at home, she did attend all our piano recitals. I was sure the year that I was afflicted with a nasty case of poison ivy I could get out of the recital. Mom would not relent, so while waiting for my turn to play my memorized piece in the auditorium, I sat with a tissue and blotted up the weeping-ivy blisters between my fingers. The unsightly blisters also covered my legs; I felt like a leprosy victim right out of the Old Testament. There was an empty seat on each side of me; my fellow piano students had probably read about those Bible lepers.

The shunning did nothing for my nervous butterflies. I really thought it was cruel and unusual punishment to make me appear in public, on stage, looking so horrid. No daughter could think more evil thoughts of her mother than I could as I sat there ashamed of my hideous, weeping skin. Well, I showed her. When my time came, I marched onto the stage, sat myself down at the intimidating grand piano and performed perfectly. My rendition of "Greensleeves" never sounded better. I bowed proudly at the edge of the stage, and confidently marched back to my chair. Not once did I hear a word of praise from Mom for being so brave and performing so well. Is it any wonder there is so much angst in me over music?

I tried a stringed instrument in my teens after meeting a girl at summer camp who sang and played the ukulele as if she belonged with the group, Peter, Paul and Mary. Dad proudly came home with a ukulele for me and I was sure this was going to be my instrument. I was going to strum and sing my way to the stage. The ukulele had a shorter life than the accordion.

I've tried in my adult life to get beyond all that angst. My husband and I fell in love with Bluegrass music and decided to incorporate it in our lives. He went back to the guitar and I decided to try the mandolin. My attempts to strum and sing were coming along pretty well, so I decided to surprise Mom and Dad with a song during a visit a few years ago. Halfway through my performance, Mom got up and walked out of the room. To be fair to her, she was well into her Alzheimer's by then. Nonetheless, I felt the disappointment of my abysmal music talent.

I have little time for the mandolin this winter. My brain and hands are busy enough with all the routines that I've established as caregiver. Every evening I give Mom a foot massage. It calms her and signals the "nighty night" portion of her brain to kick in gear. She knows that after the massage there is no more getting out of the chair, no more drinks of water, no more "let me kiss Dad one more time." She's in bliss through the entire massage but tonight it was especially good. "OH!" she said, "The way you rub your fingers all over my feet feels like you're playing the piano. All the notes are important and you are hitting all the right keys. I have music coming out of my toes."

I sat stunned. Guess my musical talent isn't quite as abysmal as I thought. It's been over 40 years since my last piano performance, but I finally received a long-deserved compliment. Tomorrow night I'll try tickling her toes with "Greensleeves."

*Photo courtesy of the Katie Frostic collection*

Starting from the top: Gwen, Dennis, Gordon, and Katie with Nip our Brittney Spaniel. Or, could it be Nip's brother Tuck? We had the brothers, Nip and Tuck, for several years. Dad always came up with interesting names for our pets and farm machinery.

# 18

# You Were The Bravest

The end of February is pocked with life ending events that unravel the last pitiful vestiges of my parent's lives. Dad's dialysis treatments are a huge disappointment. His sessions keep him alive but he has no life. He tackles everything he does with slow, calculated precision; he can dress himself, manage his personal hygiene, and eat. On a good day, he might have enough oomph to read. He hasn't trusted himself behind the wheel of a car for two months. He can no longer walk; a pivot from walker to wheelchair is a frightening experience for all of us. The cane he used for years sits in a corner growing cobwebs. A three-wheeled bike he rode a month ago sits under the awning glaring at us like a bad joke. I want to beat it with Dad's useless cane.

My parents are like converging lines coming together in the distance. They are bound to meet each other at the end.

Mom is returning to her early childhood on a speeding train. When I change her underwear, she cries and kicks her feet, "But I like these panties," as if I've slipped off her favorite pair of polka dot training pants. She is sleeping more frequently at home and at day care: 18 of 24 hours are spent in an Alzheimer's doze. The big, bad wolf knocking at our door comes disguised as pressure sores.

I beg Mom to walk with me. "I can't find my legs," she tells me.

She has fallen twice. We add more handrails, she clings to them as if they are long lost children.

It was not so long ago that she worried the neighbors when she walked, in a daze, to the corner and back. She couldn't sit still while the three of us, Dad, Mom and I, waited in a small doctor's office. She paced back and forth like a worried ant. We were so used to her pacing and nervous activity that we didn't notice when she opened the door and looked out. She didn't catch our attention until she yelled, "Does anyone know we're waiting in here!"

I wish she could still pace. I long for the Mom who had enough fight in her to be perturbed.

When she sleeps, cruel images fly across the screen of her toddler brain. "I'm having dreams of people being frozen into ice chunks," she tells me.

Her eyes beg for an explanation. She's afraid of being cold, and she worries we will abandon her. Huddled under her warm blanket on the way to day care, she stuttered, "I'm afraid when you put me in the car, you're going to take me someplace and never come back to get me."

"Mom, you don't need to worry, I will never leave you." She's quiet for several minutes and I think she's relaxed and at ease, then she breaks the silence with a soft, pathetic plea: "*Promise.*"

Her innocent, childlike comments bruise my emotions. I'm tempted to run from the pain, but with Mom in the bowels of Alzheimer's, where could I possibly go to escape? There are no hiding places. Oddly, the greatest place of comfort is here, next to her.

I reach over and squeeze her hand, "I promise I will never leave you." She squeezes back. I'm glad she can't comprehend that soon she is the one who will be leaving me.

As her disease progresses she tells me more and more that she loves me. I'm suddenly "the best daughter," she wants to hug me. She tells me that I'm sweet. There are brief, selfish moments where I wish she had died when my emotions for her had dried up. Our mother and daughter relationship always felt like sandpaper. We only knew how to rub each other wrong. We were too much alike and recoiled at our worst, shared traits. I love her again and the imminent parting is going to really sting.

"*Hold on, hold on to yourself. This is going to hurt like hell.*" This line from a Sarah McLachlan song haunts me. I scramble to make up for lost time; I'm determined to be a dedicated daughter—a "Daughter Teresa," if that could be possible.

During the few hours that she's conscious, I encourage her to exercise her brain. She can still cut out baby bibs, but the joy in it is gone from her. It's reminiscent of the way I begrudgingly practiced the piano. Unless she asks, we don't do bibs any more. She can't stand long enough to help me make cookies or jam, so I pull out a photo album, which Katie made recently. I wonder if she knew what a useful tool this would become. Hospice volunteers who visit Mom sit next to her as she tells them her life stories. The pictures are her stage props. The old-familiar photos are a kindle for her brain; the memories, a soothing ointment.

The album begins with a picture of Mom and Dad in their teens, and then travels towards us in time. Our baby pictures sidle up next to each other in the order of our birth.

"Oh look," Mom points, "there's Katie."

She passes my picture and points out Dennis, then Gordon. I point to the fuzzy, black-and-white Polaroid of myself: My baby face is the only one not preserved with a professional photo.

"Who's this?" I ask.

"Hmm", she thinks, "I don't recognize that person."

She could just as well stab me in the heart. I want to grab and shake her while yelling, "It's me! The one who's been wiping your butt, combing your hair, rubbing your bed sores, preparing your meals!"

Shame on me. "It's not about YOU anymore, Gwen," I say to myself. We have been warned that Alzheimer's caregivers often fall ill themselves—both physically and mentally. It's true. I'm living proof.

We continue to look though the album. Four O'Leary children smile at us from moments snapped years ago. From the age of three, I towered over my older sister. Even in adulthood my younger brothers never reached my height. When we were little tykes, Dad loved to pose us by birth order; if it weren't for me, we would have been perfect stair steps.

"Look, Mom, I'm never the oldest, but I'm always the tallest."

She turns a page. We look at a silly photo of all four

of us posed on a ladder. I'm at the top; the boys are in the middle, Katie's at the bottom. Mom's finger taps the picture, "Look, you weren't the oldest, but you were always the bravest."

I adore her for saying that.

# 19

# Mom's Seventy-Fifth Birthday

At 4:30 a.m., February 25, I am startled by the ring of my cell phone. Dad's voice, hoarse and stuttering, comes over the line. "I guess I fell out of bed."

I throw back the covers and head out the door with the phone to my ear, I hurriedly make my way across the lawn in my bare feet. "I'm coming Dad, I'm on my way."

I find him lying on the floor next to the bed. He has soiled himself. I fight back my tears as I rush to gather cleaning supplies. He has always been fastidious about his hygiene; I know he's mortified and ashamed.

When I get him tucked in bed, he looks at me with heartbreaking eyes, "Have you ever felt so helpless?"

I pat him on the shoulder and answer, with a bit of a grin, hoping to touch his funny bone, "Yeah, when I gave birth."

He laughs with me and I give him a hug thinking all is well.

All is *not* well. Before the clock strikes six, Dad suffers from another bout of diarrhea. This time after cleaning him, I crawl in bed next to him and hold on tight. We both feel helpless. I pat him like a baby. I'm too scared to talk. He's too weak to voice his fears.

All is getting worse right before my eyes and I naively think I can still pull off Mom's birthday party. Guests are arriving in the afternoon for pizza. Uncle Herb is bringing his famous apple pie. I have presents wrapped. As Mom would say, "Come hell or high water" we're going to celebrate. We didn't celebrate. At 10:00 a.m., Dad is on the way to the hospital in an ambulance.

Since Mom's symptoms started over ten years ago, Dad has been the unsung hero. He's been the force that has kept her steady. He chose dialysis not for his own life, but to be there for her. It doesn't take long for Mom to crumble without his constant presence. We take her to the hospital for visits, but she gets nervous and asks to go home after 15 minutes. Once she's home she constantly asks, "Where's Gerald?"

We use a card communication device that we've used in the past to ease her anxiety. On 5x7 cards, we've written:

*Gerald is at dialysis, Lon will drive him home.*
*Gerald is at physical therapy, Gwen will pick him up.*
*Phyllis is coming today to give you a shower.*

We add a new card:
*Gerald is in the hospital. He'll be home in a few days.*
We spread the cards around the house like platters of

hors d'oeuvre's, waiting for guests to arrive. She's dubious about the new message and all the other lies we tell in a feeble effort to pacify her anxiety.

Finally, she snaps, "Is he hanging with another woman?"

Her paranoia is nothing new, last winter she accused *me* of having an affair with Dad.

I almost burst out laughing, but her look of fear and suspicion helped pull me together. "No, Mom, he's not having an affair. He's too much in love with you."

It's comforting to finally be able to use *truth* to soothe her. I'm as weary of my incorrigible lies as she.

I move over to my parent's home and live with Mom, hoping we will be temporary roommates. Suddenly our lives feel as if we are whirling about in a blender. Instead of coming home, Dad is admitted to a skilled care facility. His medical needs are too extreme for home care; he's going to need numerous physical therapy sessions before he can walk again. Meanwhile, Mom is spared a vigorous virus running through Zephyrhills. I'm the one who spends a night vomiting. I tearfully call Lon and give him the bad news; he rushes over, and now becomes Mom's caregiver. As I lay helpless in bed, I hear her call out, "Is there any female in the house who can help me pull up my pants?"

I listen as Lon calmly talks to her as he gets her dressed. "Gwen," I say to myself, "you will never complain to this man again about the toothpaste spit he leaves in the sink. He's in there pulling up your mom's pants." What a guy. He earns so many brownie points with his kindness; he's set for life.

Hospice comes to our rescue by providing five days of respite care. The hospice house they place Mom in is stunning: fresh flowers brighten her room; her bathroom is twice the size of the little trailer we live in while on the road. The caregivers tend to her like she's long-lost royalty.

But I pity both Mom and Lon as he describes the scene when he dropped her off.

"You aren't family. You have no right to leave me here," she yelled at him. "You are half the man my husband is. Who do you think you are taking charge?" And finally when she could think of no more insults, she yelled, "You need a haircut!" He might have deserved that last comment since I am his personal barber and I've neglected his pleas for a trim.

The same day Mom arrives home, I take her to the rehabilitation center to visit Dad. They both need to see each other. As I watch them hug, hold hands, and stare silently in each other's eyes, I am dumb struck. "My gosh," I think to myself, "they're saying goodbye, they both *know*."

Sometimes as I watch them look at each other they have shocked looks on their faces, as if silently saying, "My goodness, look at us. We were just kids, in love, we had babies. What's happened?"

One time, I caught Mom out of the corner of my eye. "Mom! Did I just see you wink at Dad?"

"Well, he just winked at me," she said in self-defense.

They are like two love-struck teenagers. Trying to give them the privacy they deserve, I settle Mom in a chair next to Dad. "I'll be back in a bit. I'm going to go talk to the nurse," I say in pretense.

When I return, I stop outside the door before breaking in on them and hear Mom talking, "...don't worry, it's all in the past. Whatever we did or didn't do doesn't matter now. It's all history."

It's hard to believe she is afflicted with Alzheimer's. She is so profound. Her speech, usually interrupted with starts and stops, is precise.

Warm, spring weather comes with the month of March; it affords us the opportunity to take Dad out of the facility for fresh air. Mom can't walk more than a few yards, so Lon and I each take a parent. Side by side, as they hold hands, we wheel them around the grounds. I'm not sure who benefits most from the experience. My good intentions are meant for them, but I take great comfort in the hand holding, the winking, and the sly smiles they share. As I watch my parents say goodbye, every cell of my being is infused with emotions, more than I thought a body could embrace. It's beautiful, immense, and powerful. It fills me with energy and strips me raw in one fell swoop.

April is just around the corner. My "tour of duty" is almost over. Kate and I have many conversations about when and how we will transport our parents back to Michigan. I don't want to let them go, but I'm physically and emotionally spent. Dad is suffering with edema and pneumonia. He has no appetite, his diarrhea persists. His dialysis treatments cause his blood pressure to drastically plummet; the treatments must stop and he's not getting properly dialyzed. Dad's needs, and Mom's, pull at me from two desperate poles. I struggle to keep them alive and comfortable. I selfishly wish, upon a belligerent star, their lives be taken.

Does Dad know I wish on stars? Maybe so. It is he who chooses to end his life. "I'm done with dialysis," he tells me.

"Dad, your body is so depleted you will only survive a couple days." He nods his head.

I continue, "Once you're gone, you know Mom will soon follow."

He looks at me squarely, "I know."

I take a deep breath. In this moment, Alzheimer's is my friend, and Mom's. She dozes peacefully in her chair, unaware of the conversation taking place. I'm thankful for the oblivion her disease grants her, when she wakes, she doesn't remember that Dad is home, the hospice bed in the living room does not catch her attention.

With all the strength I can muster I keep my tears away from Dad's eyes and tell him, "I'm so proud of you, and honor your decision." Then ask, "Dad, are you scared?"

His resolute answer will be with me forever, his blue, blue eyes hold mine. "Absolutely not," he says.

Without sobbing or remorse, we embrace each other like two old war heroes who know when it's time to say goodbye and seek separate sunsets.

When I pull back and look at him, I ask one more question, "Dad, can I get you anything?"

Without hesitation he leans back, settles comfortably in his chair and smiles, "Yes, I think I'll have a bowl of ice cream."

# 20

# Where's Gerald?

Dad's decision to end dialysis keeps our family's cell phones busy as the news passes. Aunt Mary, the baby sister who swung in the hammock, arrives at the front door and whispers when she sees Dad lying in bed. "Tonight I'm bringing lasagna and salad over for dinner. Tomorrow I'll bring chicken and I also have a pork chop supper planned."

I hug her as I think, "Mary must have taken 'help' lessons from Uncle Herb."

"I don't know how else to help," she tells me.

I assure her, she certainly does know how to help.

"What else can I do?" she asks.

"Flowers," I say, "I have a few, but I want the room filled with flowers."

Her eyes brighten; Aunt Mary loves bouquets and has a generous flower budget.

Within the hour, I have a room full of blooms. As

Dad floats in and out of consciousness, he won't see the medical equipment hiding behind the bouquets.

My father always bought my mother bouquets. He would arrive home with a big smile and fresh flowers. Saturday mornings, on the way home from his night shift at the GM foundry in Saginaw, he would pick Kate and I up from piano lessons. Each of us would choose a flowering plant or bouquet for Mom. Several times this winter, he has requested, "How about a fresh bouquet for Mom."

I tuck him under one of Mom's favorite quilts; roses, lilies, and hyacinths fill the room with a promising, spring fragrance even though we know all the promises for Dad are over.

Katie and Del arrive from Michigan before Dad is permanently unconscious. In the next 48 hours, we all lean on each other and figure out how to play our parts in the last episode of Dad's life. It's a surreal experience to go about daily activities—put food on the table, take out the trash, collect the mail, tend to Mom, greet visitors, and converse with hospice—while Dad lies dying. Thankfully, Mom is composed; as she passes him on the way to the shower, she pats his hand, then looks at me and says, "Don't bother him, he's sleeping."

When the hands of the clock move into the first minutes of Good Friday, Dad is no longer with us.

The room is tranquil as Kate and I discuss how to tell Mom. Mortuary personnel will arrive soon. Do we wake her and tell her that Dad is dead, and let her see his body? We want her to say her last goodbyes as we have. To *not* give this opportunity seems cruel, but to *facilitate* it seems heartless. She has the brain of a child and the shock of seeing him will frighten her. She won't *remember* she's seen him or said her sad goodbyes. Alzheimer's robs her of a final parting, but also protects her from immense grief.

"But, Katie, what will we do when she asks about him."

"We'll cross that bridge when we come to it," she says confidently.

While Mom slumbers, I administer a liquid medication from hospice under her tongue to keep her in a deep sleep. When the mortuary service arrives, she will be our Sleeping Beauty, far off in a fairytale land where people don't die and love never ends.

Less than 24 hours after Dad's death, Mom's legs completely give out. Even with the commode next to her chair, it is frightfully difficult for Kate and me to maneuver her from one to the other. Her legs wobble, there is no support, and a simple, pivot move is an immense struggle. Kate and I look at each other wide-eyed. Both of us silently say, "My gosh, she's going quick."

I loose my hold on Mom as I try to ease her down in her chair. She sinks in a powerful plop. "Mom, are you OK? Are you comfortable?"

She stares up at both of us, and in a snap replies, "Well, considering the positions you've had me in lately, I feel pretty damn good."

To the end, she makes us burst with laughter.

The last time I see Mom totally conscious she is sitting in the front seat of the car. Lon is driving Kate, Del, and Mom to the airport to catch a last minute flight to Michigan. Mom is snuggled under her warm blanket, her hair is freshly styled, lipstick and rouge disguise her wasted and depleted body. I blow kisses to her and then hold my crossed arms over my chest to mime a hug. She smiles sweetly and struggles to get her hands from under the blanket. Grinning, she holds up her hands, and like a baby, she wiggles her fingers at me: a perfectly executed, last goodbye.

Once Mom is settled at Kate's home in Michigan, she finally asks. "Where's Gerald?"

Katie stands next to the bed and slowly begins, "Well, Mom, you know Dad was very sick, his dialysis wasn't working and his body…"

"Is he dead?" Mom asks.

Katie squeezes Mom's hand and softly replies, "Yes, Mom. Dad's dead."

Mom doesn't really cry, but her eyes fill with tears. She gives a huge shoulder-dropping sigh and says, "I guess that means I'm a widow now."

Mom is bedridden but she fights for her freedom. She demands to be allowed out of bed. She refuses to urinate in her disposable briefs. To get her on the commode is dangerous, so Kate resorts to a bedpan.

"I want to walk," she demands.

Kate gets her to the side of the bed and allows Mom to try and use her legs. It's futile. As Kate helps Mom lie back, she looks at Kate with big, brown, doe eyes and asks, "Will I ever walk again? Will I ever get better? Am I going to die?"

Katie gets into bed next to Mom and snuggles close. Her voice can't help but crack, "Yes, Mom. You're dying."

As if she's a small child who doesn't want to feel any pain, Mom looks at Katie, stares into her eyes, and tells her, "I hope it happens fast."

In the last weeks of Dad's life, Mom often commented, "It's time for me to go." When Dad was in the hospital, away from her, she clearly stated to me several times, "I'll never live alone." Can people will themselves to let go, give the disease the upper hand and stop fighting?

When I arrived in Michigan to help Katie with Mom, I finally met part of the support team that assisted my sister last summer. I had heard about Pam, who would sit with Mom under the shade of an old, oak tree at a local park and read her *Little House on the Prairie*. Now, here she was greeting me as if I were a long lost sister.

I watched as Janice caressed and soothed Mom; as if, this was her own mother who lay dying. Janice showed more love towards my mother—who was now an empty shell—than even I, her own flesh and blood, could muster.

Vicki, who not only helped with Mom, but also took over office responsibilities for Katie, knew more about my sister's life and what assistance she needed than I did. These women made my inner most spirit weep with gratitude for all they gave.

Where would Katie and I be without our support teams? How would I have survived the last five months in Florida without my hospice team?

Where would we be without the local Alzheimer's association, Walk To Remember, that provided financial support when Katie needed respite care?

While Katie was in Florida helping me with Dad, her support team in Michigan cleaned, prepared meals, and greeted my sister when she arrived home with our dying mother.

Kristy, Kate and Del's minister's wife, can read the silent cries for help in my sister's face. Most people see in my sister, what they saw in my mother, strength and confidence. Kristy knows when there's a slight crack in

Katie's armor, and can help her fight the battles. My mother, in her "Alzheimer's speak," would have said, "It's a good thing Kristy's in the same rowboat as Katie."
There were so many people who helped us row our boat. It takes a community of family, friends, and professional organizations if you are to survive the storm that life-ending diseases bring.

Only a week had passed since Mom waved goodbye to me in Florida, but now as I walked to her bed, I saw a decade of impending death hanging heavily on her face. I sat next to Mom and held her hand. As she slipped in and out of consciousness, she seemed to know I was there. Her last question to me as she clutched my hand, was, "Are you leaving?"

"No, Mom," I squeezed back, "I'm not leaving, I'm staying."

She closed her eyes and rested.

I believe she knew all along that she was the one who would soon be leaving.

# 21

# Alzheimer's Last Gift

Throughout our lives, my sister and I agreed on only a few things: yeast makes bread rise, and sunsets occur in the west. Religion and politics were topics we danced around like two barnyard hens; each waiting to defend our position should the other one peck. Our lives took us on extremely divergent paths before we exited our teens. As the years cranked forward, we haphazardly shared birthday cards and Christmas greetings. I moved west and raised my children in the shadows of the San Juan Mountains in Colorado; Kate raised hers near the shores of Lake Huron only a few miles from our childhood home in Michigan. We had the same parents, but not the same childhood. Animosity did not describe our sisterhood, but neither did companionship.

Alzheimer's changed our fractured sisterhood. Mom's disease was so devastating her daughters had but one moral choice—to work as a team and give Mom the dignity she deserved. After years of emotional and geographic space between us, we found the same path and took a beautiful journey together with someone we shared, our mom.

When I cared for Mom, I would call Sis and weep with frustration when Mom would slam the door in my face or when I found another drawer of unpaid bills.

When Kate was in charge, she would describe what it was like to live with Mom. Kate and Del never knew what would set Mom off in a rage. Most irritating, was Mom shadowing Katie throughout the day as she helped manage the farm, her salon business, and her private duty companion home care business. We consoled each other, planned how to manage Mom's disease, and shared the hope of Mom dying before she would forget our faces and names.

Sis and I shared three years as tag team caregivers. We concentrated on Mom's needs and discovered the peculiar little ways we were alike. Hard physical work in times of stress is our friend, chores have to be done before we can recreate, and beds are made before breakfast is on the table. All these habits germinated during our early days on the farm under Mom's guidance. Neither of us realized how deeply they had taken root in our personalities.

In Mom's last week, we stood facing each other as she lay comatose between us and discovered another point of agreement. Mom was no longer with us; she still took shallow breaths and her body was legally alive, but for us, the *real* Donna was gone. The only thing about her that still existed was in us, two sisters, two daughters, who would continue to carry bits and pieces of her character and temperament. The essence of our mother now remained in us.

For several days, we each held Mom's hand and urged her to join Dad. "He's waiting for you," "It's time to go now," "You don't need to hang on for us."

It seemed like a poorly directed movie where Mom refused to play the part of a dead woman. Our script, our words, none of it worked.

Katie looked at me and said, "She's as stubborn as you are." We broke into fits of laughter, because we both knew it to be true.

"Let's try reverse physiology," I suggested.

Katie's eyebrows rose, "How?"

I stood at the end of Mom's bed, grabbed her feet, and said, "Mom, I'm going to the bathroom. Don't die until I get back. OK?"

Kate understood my need for humor, but our husbands thought we were getting too close to insanity's border.

Sis defended what looked like cold callousness, "We've been saying goodbye to our mother for a long time. The person in this bed is a shell of the person who raised us. She's a breathing corpse, we've already grieved, and humor is one way for us to get through this hideous ending." I loved Kate for saying that.

We kept a 24/7 deathbed vigil. Mom was left alone for only brief moments, but we listened to every breath with the aid of a baby monitor. Ironic, isn't it, that the beginnings and endings of life are so closely monitored when what really counts is the life that's lived between?

We walked a balance beam of frightful indecision; we wanted Mom's suffering to end but for that wish to be granted meant death. We laid fresh hyacinths from Katie's garden on Mom's pillow and covered her with one of Dad's favorite western shirts. We sat next to her as we wrote thank you cards in response to the memorial service we held for Dad just days previous. Actually, it was a double memorial. Mom became comatose the day before Dad's service and Katie and I came to another point of agreement. Mom would be dead in a few days and neither of us had the physical or emotional strength to plan another funeral. While standing over Mom's rigid but breathing body, we both agreed that tomorrow at 2 p.m., alive or dead, Mom would be included in the memorial.

Four days later Mom's breathing was so automated and mechanical I called her "Ventilator Mommy" for the sound she made. The first time she stopped breathing we rushed to her side, urgently calling out to Del and Lon, "Come quick, this is it, she's going."

Katie put her hand on Mom's forehead and she started breathing again.

"Next time she stops breathing, don't touch her," I demanded. "I think it revived her."

"OK, no more touching," Katie agreed.

Lon looked at us with dilated, owl eyes. "You girls are sick".

The two of us stood elbow-to-elbow as if a single entity and retorted back, "No we're not, we're just ready for our mother to be at peace."

But of course, we continued to touch and kiss and stroke and whisper our love as Mom slowly continued her journey towards Dad.

On Mom's last night I sat and watched her chest rise and fall. Next to her sat a black box containing Dad's ashes. The weeping and sadness had long since drained out of me and in that moment, I felt peaceful serenity. When I described this odd sense of tranquility to Kate, she gave me a great compliment. "Gwen, it's because you were able to embrace death, not many people have that ability."

Sis and I are finally sisters again; real sisters, companions even, and we agree on one more thing:

Mom would be proud.

*Photo courtesy of the Katie Frostic collection*

Donna Jean Bloom O'Leary
She was strong, independent, and stunning. Dad always
boasted, "I took one look at your mother and it was love
at first sight."

# Looking Back

*Three days after my parents arrived in Florida, I sent an email to Katie describing the day's activities. It sounds busy and bumbling; I had so much to learn. I'm glad I didn't know what I was getting into and I'm not sorry I stayed.*

*I have not revised this letter except to add or change a few words for clarity. You can tell by the clipped sentences that my time was limited. This is what life was like everyday. What a RIDE!*

What did we do in Zhills today?

Dad took Mom to breakfast way out in the Hardees area to Rick's Cafe. It's an old haunt of theirs—a place where a guy used to play a fiddle for entertainment.

Returned the baby monitor and bought bigger panties for Mom and new night lights, also made keys for Lon and me to carry—to open/lock our laundry room.

Booster seat came for the toilet. She loves it.

Took Mom to get her hearing aid fixed. New tube, no more beep beep—picked up her two jackets at dry cleaners on the way home. All the while "where are we going...."

LPN came for a visit after we got home

Meals on Wheels came

Social worker came--long visit with lots of questions for me. Mom was sleeping most of the time. Sent Lon and Dad to Dialysis because Social Worker was taking so long. Lon called and informed me I had sent them one hour early. Shot myself in the head with fake pistol. At least they got the paper work done, then came home for an hour rest.

Dr. Patel called just about the time I needed to take Dad back to Dialysis. Lon, smart man, took it upon himself to take Dad and do the dialysis duty without me. I went to relieve Lon in just a couple minutes but Dad got in right away so my efforts were for naught.

Took Mom for a pedicure. Her toenails were starting to grow into the skin so I told her she needed this done every month. She actually wanted COLOR on her toes.

Mom just walked by. I told her I was writing to you. "Hello Katie" is what she said. She actually knew that I would send this over the internet without me prompting!!!!!!!!

She has paced ever since we got home with new toes. No way could she be left alone like last year.

SMART girl I am for buying a NetBook, and iTouch, and for having good reading on hand for all the hours I will spend here. At least it smells good and our temps today not so horrid. I actually had to get an extra blanket this morning to finish out my last snooze before making coffee.

I think all is under control. We've walked together twice today and she actually has seemed to like it.

Dad signed the DNR
*(Katie and I feared he would not sign the 'Do Not Resuscitate' order for Mom.)*

Gotta go, she decided to go walking down the street and its dark.

Hugs
How's Del?

This is not a book with 'How To' tips. It is simply my mother's story. Many professionals will be able to guide you should your family be challenged with an Alzheimer's diagnosis. I only offer my Sister's advice, "Find something to laugh about every day;" otherwise, the heartache will cripple you.

# Farm Stories

As my parents aged, gift giving occasions became challenging. They had everything they needed. Instead of trinkets or flowers, I wrote stories of our life on the farm and presented them as gifts.

These are the stories I gave to Dynamic Seniors. Mom would sit and listen intently and sometimes interrupted to add further descriptions, or point out a detail I may have missed. She loved having them read to her, more so, I think she loved being the main character.

*Photo courtesy of the Katie Frostic collection*

From left to right: Katie, Gordon, Gwen and Dennis

We proudly posed for Dad in what we called, "A *clean* field of beans." We would often take drives on Sunday afternoon to see how other crops in the neighborhood were growing. We were always judgmental and quick to comment if someone hadn't hoed their beans. We lived the life you hear about in the lyrics of Bluegrass music.

# 22

# Bean Summer Mornings

Our 140 acres of Michigan farm was home, work, play and the only life we O'Leary children knew, aside from our school and church activities. Dad worked seven days a week at General Motors in Saginaw 60 miles away, leaving Mom with many of the farm responsibilities. A half-mile off M46, on Fitch Road, we raised primarily wheat and beans with a few crops of oats, corn, and sugar beets. Our white navy bean plants had beautiful green, heart-shaped leaves, but their beauty was deceiving. They needed weeding and it was a labor-intensive job. After several decades, I still have vivid memories of bean summer mornings.

Hoeing weeds was a family affair led by Mom. She would wake all four of us before dawn for a cold cereal and milk breakfast. We were out in the fields just as the sun started its steady climb up the sky. Michigan's hot humid environment is gruesome and hard labor was reserved for cool, early morning hours when fog hung heavy in the air. The bean plants were less than a foot high when we started the weeding season. If we neglected the crop, the weeds would hog the resources: without water, space, and sun, there would be no crop. It was a simple equation: no crop, no cash income. As a kid, I hated hoeing those beans. As an adult, I cherish those times. I can picture my mom as she led a pack of four reluctant, complaining, farm kids. Recounting the experience brings back pleasant memories and lessons learned.

This is what it looked like:

You would stand in the middle of a row of beans with a row to your right and left. Mom would have two or three rows on each side of her, then she would place Dennis and Gordon on each side of her rows; they were the youngest and needed the most supervision. Katie and I would be off to the side of the boys. As a group we would weed a swath of beans about 16 to 20 rows wide depending on how weedy the fields were and how many rows we could each manage. If it wasn't too weedy, Kate and I could each handle several rows like Mom. After we got down to the end of the field, we would position ourselves into a new set of bean rows and back we would head to where we started.

It took us about a half hour to do one round trip. It all depended on how long the rows, how weedy the field, how crabby and lazy we were, and how hot and tired we became. We always worked as a group following Mom's cadence. She worked hard, fast, and sweated like a horse, a trait she added to any job she ever took for the rest of her life. We all learned to march to her rhythm; she was our drumbeat. We didn't always march happily. There where constant complaints of being hot, tired, and thirsty. Mom was no fool; she carried pitchers of cold Kool-Aid to the fields along with slabs of her homemade bread and jam.

The hoes were always in good condition, their blades always razor slick. We would stick them in a vise in Dad's workshop and slide a sharpening file back and forth until the ragged, dirty edge was sharp and shiny. Mom would carry a file to the fields with her and sharpen any dull edges during the work hours. The trick to weeding is to remove the entire weed, root and all, from the soil. You had to do this while reaching around the tender stems of the bean plants with the blade of the hoe. To get the whole weed, without damaging a bean was a skill we all proudly acquired. However, not before we each had secretly hoed out a few bean plants. If you were quick enough, and clever enough, you could get the bean "replanted" before anyone saw your error.

The straight rows of beans and consistent height were striking. The weeds that shot above the beans were markedly visible, like a bad hair day, country-style. The weeds had their own characteristics. Pigweeds have a tough stalk and were difficult to remove if you didn't get to them in their youth when the stalk was soft and pliable. Ragweed has a frilly leaf structure, and were easy to whack at any age. Burdock is a weed similar to cast iron. Mom would always come to the rescue if your rows had a bully patch of burdock.

If we didn't get to a field early in the season, the weeds would be difficult to hoe. We would have to pull the larger weeds to get the entire root. In those instances, we would send Dennis and Gordon ahead. They loved to meander among our rows, jumping and running to stay ahead of us, as we concentrated on the smaller weeds.

Pulling the weeds in tandem was a game for the boys.

The bigger the weed, the more difficult the tug, and thus the harder they would tumble to the ground. The spray of dirt as the earth finally relinquished the root was an added treat for my rough and tumble farm brothers. A rivulet of sweat rolling down through the grime on their faces was their badge of honor. The dirtier they got, the greater the fun. Sometimes we would cover the thick green stalk with our 8 hands and in "quadratic O'Leary power" yank out a behemoth weed. It would send us in a backward rumble of kids, weeds, dirt, and sweat. We seldom wore gloves so we all earned wonderful, thick patches of calluses before the hoeing season ended.

In the weediest fields, it was always a treat to look back on the rows as we worked. The perfect lines of beans were like soldiers standing at command. We were proud of our achievement. Mom would give a report to Dad with details on what field we had hoed, how much we had accomplished, how weedy the field was, and how well the crop was growing. We have a photo in our family album where all four of the O'Leary kids stand side by side, each between a row of beans in a field we had finished hoeing. The beans were bushy and bountiful that year and Dad wanted to capture our moment of pride. It seems almost laughable doesn't it? Some people might snicker and say, "Wow, you O'Leary's really knew how to have fun." Indeed, we did. It's a fine lesson to learn there is joy in the toil of daily life.

After one long, hot morning of hoeing, I was relishing the thought of cooling my feet in the small pool we erected every summer. While hanging our hoes in Dad's work shed, Katie came up to me and whispered, "Want to surprise Mom and Dad?" "Sure," I answered, thinking maybe we were going to buy them something with our babysitting money. "What should we buy?"

"No, we're not going to *buy* anything; we're going to *do* something."

"What?"

"Let's go back to the field and finish the last rows we didn't get hoed."

I looked at her in disgust. She was asking me to work with the sun high in the sky. We were hot and sweaty and she wanted to go back!

"Come on", she cajoled. "It'll be fun. It'll be a great surprise."

I didn't tread out to the field because I was kind and wanted to help. I didn't join her because I was suddenly awash with high purpose ideals. I went along *only* because I knew she would head out there without me and garner all the eventual praise. We had to walk a quarter of a mile to get to the field and then spent an hour completing the job. It wasn't as bad as I thought; it actually *was* fun. It was the first time I experienced going above what was expected. The feeling afterwards was rewarding, even better than all the praise Mom and Dad offered. It was a valuable lesson and I owe it all to a sister and a field of beans.

I can close my eyes today and visualize those green rows of plants that took me out of bed on early summer mornings. The fruits of our labor were always immediate with many of our farm chores. When we finished the early fieldwork, we would head home to a day of less rigorous chores and play. My brothers and I would climb the Catalpa trees, romp in the haymow, or try to catch frogs in the ditch. Katie and I might head out for a bike ride on back roads or spend time on sewing projects. To this day, I do my least favorable chore first. When it's done and out of the way, my life feels tidy and my remaining hours aren't cluttered with the knowledge of a waiting responsibility.

Those early mornings on the Michigan farm, following Mom's work tempo, set a standard that I incorporated in my career and home life. The bean field work ethic my mother taught me provided a firm foundation in my life and has served me well.

Thanks Mom for teaching by example and being proud of my accomplishments.

# 23

# Riding Ollie

I love living in the west; the desert is my home. I call it red rock country. I was smitten with red rock landscape when I was first introduced on a backpacking trip in southern Utah. Hiking through towering, narrow corridors, you can almost hear grand geologic stories, as the wind slices along red sandstone, slowly eroding the walls one tiny grain of sand at a time. I'm jealous of those who share their childhood with this incredible geology.

The geology of my childhood is not red sandstone. I come from land scoured by glaciers. Smooth, rounded rocks left from retreating glaciers were plentiful on our Michigan farm. They popped out against the dark, loamy soil in our fields like Easter eggs every time one of Michigan's long spring rains would wash the land, erode the soil around the rocks, and expose their millennial hiding place. I cursed those rocks for the toil it took to remove them from our fields.

People in corn country say you can hear the corn grow. You could lie awake at night and hear the sound of rocks rising through the soil on our farm. The rocks seemed to push themselves out of the soil and reach for the light as if giant seeds competing against the tiny seeds we planted as a cash crop.

We had to clear the rocks from the fields. "They'll get caught in the disks of the tiller," Dad explained, "or get stuck between the plow blades, or snag the tines of the harvesting combine."

Rocks, picked up miles from here by a slow-moving glacier, were deposited as the glacier melted. We, The O'Leary Clan, would pick them up and move them again.

Before spring planting we would hitch a flatbed trailer to our old, green Oliver tractor—"Ollie," we called it, "Ollie Oliver." We all loved driving Ollie and looked forward to our turn at the wheel as if it were a ride at the county fair. We would slowly drive Ollie through the field as the entire family walked on each side and behind the trailer. Our swaths down the field were as wide as possible. Down to the end of the field, we would trudge, gathering rocks, then, after a quick break at the end, we would turn and head back.

Every 20 minutes, over Ollie's chugging and deafening engine, we would yell for the driver to stop so the next kid could have a turn at the wheel. The driver, even the youngest and shortest of the brood, would reach down to step on the clutch, then the brake. Dad would hop up to shove Ollie's gear lever into neutral and the next kid would happily settle into the old, worn seat that wobbled like a loose tooth. The black steering wheel seemed as big around as a Ferris wheel. After a few minutes, my arms would ache from reaching out so wide and clutching the vibrating wheel, but I never complained. Riding Ollie was a lot easier than pick'n rocks. Everything on Ollie vibrated and shook. He was loud, dirty, and smelled of oil, grease, and sweat. We loved that old green hunk for the ride and rest he gave us.

When one of us would encounter a large rock, half buried and refusing to budge, we would yell out for the driver to stop. Mom and Dad would come over with shovels, pickaxe, and pry bar to start the excavation project. They would dig a trench along the side of the rock with shovels and axe, then, positioning the pry bar, they would grunt, heave, sweat and swear until the rock popped out like a worried, decayed molar. The two of them would heft it between them and wrestle it onto the trailer. We would watch, amazed at their strength and ability to move so well.

They waltzed their way to the flatbed with the rock between them as if our field was a dance floor. With a loud crunch, the rock would land on the warped wood; splinters of rocks and wood flew like lethal projectiles. As they stood admiring their accomplishment, the dust would start to settle, the wood moaned, and the smaller rocks jumped around like the Mexican beans we won as prizes at the county fair. As Mom wiped her brow with the back of her hand, Dad would yell for the driver to start up and on we would toil.

We had to keep up with Ollie as we spread out to gather rocks, then run to catch up as we struggled to carry our load. The fields were peppered with rocks and it was tempting to pick away at the little ones. "Don't pick up anything smaller than your head," Dad would yell out when he spied us going for the easy pickings.

There were times a section of field was so plagued with rocks I wondered why we didn't open a gravel pit rather than planting crops. We would yell out, "STOP!" to whoever was driving Ollie, then, scurrying back and forth, we would make a game of how fast we could get the area cleaned. Everyone did their part, we were all on the same team; our group effort was a country glue that bonded our family together. We all pressed on no matter how tired we became. When we finished for the day, we would plunk our tired bottoms on the trailer bed and ride through a cloud of dust as Dad drove Ollie towards our old, red barn. We were all festered with blisters, our faces smeared with dust and sweat. The boys always found the energy to haggle over who had the biggest blood blister.

Dad would park Ollie along our growing rock pike and we would unload our catch for the day. Unloading was just as brutal and dangerous as loading. Fingers could get pinched, nails were certainly broken, and we all watched out for each other's heads as we tossed, threw, and rolled rocks off the trailer. For the smaller rocks, we would bend over with our backs to the pile and start chucking rocks between our legs, making a game of the work. Finally, Dad would park Ollie in the barn and for the rest of the day we were free to play and romp as we pleased.

Years later while designing a water-wise garden for my yard in Salt Lake City, I sought out landscaping stones at my favorite rock shop. Perusing the various bins, I stopped before a mound of beautifully rounded rocks—just like the ones we plucked from our fields so many years ago. I paid dearly for them. As I strategically placed them around my flowers and shrubs, I chuckled at the image of a great rock pile still sitting next to the old, red barn back on the Michigan farm.

*Photo courtesy of the Katie Frostic collection*

Gordon and Dennis
On Ollie Oliver

# 24

# Killdeer

Growing up on the farm, I associated periods of the year with farm activities. Summer was growing season, fall was for harvesting, and winter provided a rest. Spring, my favorite time of the year, was plowing season. Mom drove Ollie, our old, lumbering, green Oliver tractor, through our fields churning the dark sleepy soil to life. The plow would scoop large swirls of dark earth squirming with perturbed earthworms. Before they could wiggle their way back to their dark caves, snowy white seagulls from Lake Huron squawked and screeched over who should have the juiciest specimen.

Scurrying among the rubble of last years crop, nervous, long-legged killdeer frantically scratched away at natural depressions in the soil. They added dried bits of vegetation and surrounded their nests with tiny pebbles as if creating a protective moat. The ground is a strange and dangerous environment for a nursery and Mom made every attempt to preserve them as she plowed.

"You can't be plowing around every nest," Dad told her, "It takes up too much land." The killdeer that noisily set up housekeeping on our little farm did not touch my father's heart as they did my mom's. These nervous, long-legged plovers were her favorite bird. She watched carefully with a keen eye for the nearly invisible nests they made in our fields.

Killdeer do not quietly step aside when you invade their territory. Upon the least intrusion, they circle around their home, haranguing invaders with screeching "dee dee dee" calls. "Exit now!" they demand. They are a noble looking bird. Soft, white bellies below rich, brown plumage on their backs make them look as if they've donned a royal cloak. Two ebony rings of feathers, like pearl necklaces, surround the necks of both male and female birds. Running swiftly on stilted legs, their movements are so fluid, they drift and hover over the ground before gliding smoothly through the air. If you're lucky enough to discover a nest with eggs, you'll see delicate, pale, buff eggs decorated with blackish-brown mottling.

The female persistently protects her rock nursery, ever watchful for dangers—like tractors pulling "sharp blades." She employs a protective maneuver by feigning injury. Dragging herself as though mortally wounded with wing bent and trailing, she coaxes predators away from her eggs or chicks. Our killdeer used this technique with Mom as she drove Ollie through our fields. With bent wing and agitated cry, one mother sent a message to another. Our mother driving the tractor listened, watched, and heeded the plight of the bird.

My mother was not an ordinary farm wife. She baked, cooked, cleaned, shopped, sewed, and decorated on a budget like many farm women in Michigan's agricultural belt. However, she also took on farm chores traditionally preformed by men. Like many Michigan farmers, Dad had a full-time job in the auto industry. He commuted 120 miles a day, seven days a week, 365 days a year. Therefore, my mother prepared the spring fields for planting, then sowed, weeded, worried and harvested. She knew how to weld and repair machinery. She was carpenter, roofer, painter and plumber, strong-bodied and strong-minded.

When Dad said, "plow up those nests," Mom solved the problem her way. With great determination, she became an expert at driving farm machinery. Using skills as intricate as those she used in sewing and knitting projects, she could thread the cumbersome farm machinery around the tiny, rock nests. We all gathered around and admired how the plow blade had churned the soil just inches from the nests with little waste of precious cropland. Dad's proud grin, the slight shake of his head, and his arm around Mom's shoulder were clear evidence she had won the battle over the nests.

Weaving the planting drill around the nests, she sowed seeds at the front doors of killdeer nurseries. The crops that soon sprung up would provide protective camouflage from predators. Later in the summer, long after the eggs had incubated, we might come across an abandoned nest as we walked through rows of bushy bean plants while hoeing weeds. We might even see pieces of broken eggs shells in the slight depression that marked where two mothers had met earlier in the spring.

Shrill cries of the killdeer's "kill-dee kill-dee" and "dee dee dee" were as common and recognizable to me as the determined mating call of robins through spring and deep, baritone songs sung by bullfrogs on hot, August nights. The sounds of nature I learned in my childhood are still with me. However, I treasure the cry of a killdeer; it brings back sweet memories of Mom on the plow, carefully weaving her way around killdeer nests.

When I moved from the farm, the call of the killdeer followed. In the mountain countryside of Colorado, I discovered a brood of baby killdeer during a spring stroll to the mailbox. I would have walked past their camouflaged bodies—they were so still—however, they responded to their mother's anxious plea to flee. A few, sharp notes were all they needed to suddenly scurry away as if one entity. Four, little, anxious birds appeared to float, rather than run, to safety.

As I learned on the farm, killdeer will build their nests in very vulnerable places: in fields, along driveways, always on the ground and always subject to predators and other dangers like tractors and even sailboats. While launching my sailboat at the Great Salt Lake, I happened upon a killdeer nest. Four, mottled eggs lay vulnerably out in the open. Sailors eager to get their boats in the water would never notice. Just like my mother, I felt a need to protect. I surrounded her tiny nest with a large ring of rocks to make it more evident. Maybe she could get those eggs incubated without incident.

I made many trips to the marina that summer to check on her; I felt personally responsible for the continuation of the species. Throughout the incubation season, the diligent mom bravely protected her eggs as cars, trucks, and sailboats on trailers scurried around the circle of rocks.

Five islands sprinkle the Great Salt Lake, the most accessible being Antelope Island with its unusual ecosystem of desert plants, various shorebirds, bison, bighorn sheep and several species of plover, including the largest—killdeer. While camping along the crusted, salt shores of Antelope Island, I spied a killdeer as she scuffled along the ground, trailing a broken wing. Her rusty tail feathers fanned out as she cried the familiar "kill-dee kill-dee." Talking gently, I reassured her that I was no threat and started to back away. The killdeer continued with her extremely agitated cry, and her broken-wing ploy was very convincing. Then I saw the real threat: A three-foot snake slithered towards her precious eggs. I chased the snake several yards from the nest, but then it slithered down a hole and I could offer no further protection.

Killdeer habitat is usually in open country: short grass prairies, golf courses, and plowed fields. However, I hear their piercing cry even in the middle of the city when I'm out gardening, running, or biking. I search the sky and ground always hoping for a glimpse of the ring-necked beauty. They continue to touch my heart, and of course, I always think of Mom.


Postscript:

When I read this to Mom two weeks before she died, she interrupted my reading and said, "Someone who knows a lot about me must have wrote this story."

Two days following Mom's death, as Lon and I made our way west, we stopped for a bike ride along the Katy Trail in Missouri. The trail is a Rails-to-Trails conversion through rolling countryside. We parked our trailer and truck in a weedy gravel lot, and, while getting ready to ride, I heard the familiar cry of an agitated killdeer. The mother killdeer treated us with her rendition of the broken-wing ploy but soon decided we were no threat and settled down to incubate while we rode off on our bikes.

She was off her nest when we returned; I cautiously made my way towards her nest and caught a glimpse of four, pale eggs, mottled with brown. Mother killdeer was not far off and quickly scolded me for getting too close, just as my mother would have scolded me. She was right; I had ventured too close to her nursery. I gave her the respect and space she deserved.

Killdeer: they'll always be my favorite bird, and they'll always bring back memories of Mom.

# And Now
# A Round Of Applause
# For:

Without the encouragement and support from my sister, Katie Frostic, this story would still be secretly hiding in my journal. Thanks, Sis, for your never-ending confidence in the story and my ability tell it. Katie is my first editor, my fact checker, my memory jogger, my agent, and manager. Without her entrepreneurial spirit and business savvy, this project would have never found its wings.

Katie *and* my brother, Gordon O'Leary, financially backed me in this book project. I am truly grateful for their generosity.

I must also thank my brother-in-law, Delmer Frostic, for the summer home he gave my parents for 29 years, for his dedication to their care, and for supporting my sister as she threw herself into this project. My thanks to you, Del, is modest compared to what you gave.

To my husband Lon Hinde: I cannot begin to tell the world what a nugget you are in my life. For seventeen years, you have listened to hundreds of my rotten first drafts, mostly while awake but sometimes in a bored slumber. You have been my best critic, my best fan, my best friend, my technical manager, and my driver. While I have fretted over deadlines on this project, you have found serene, quiet campsites in the deserts and mountains of Utah, Colorado, and New Mexico, so I could write. Thank you, my love, for giving me this beautiful life and for loving me with such depth.

Thank you Pam Surbrook, my high school chum, who was a willing participant in this project. Pam offered the first non-family eyes to this book. Decades after throwing our mortarboards in the tiny village of Carsonville, who would have thought, we would meet again this way? Thank you so much for your time and effort.

Thank you Nicola Fucigna, for agreeing to be my copy editor. From a chance meeting at Between the Covers bookshop in Telluride, Colorado, we then attended a workshop put on by authors Craig Childs and Amy Irvine. It was there I learned you had copy-editing expertise. You have offered such wise counsel and provided the Occam's Razor my writing needed. Thank you so much for your proficiency, keen eye, and dedication. I am truly grateful.

Thank you Craig Childs, for the three simple words you gave me, seven years ago in Torrey, Utah, after your tremendous workshop. You looked at me and said, "You can write." Thanks for believing in me, I'm glad I've finally learned to believe in myself.

A final word of thanks to Barbara Brunson, of Vanilla House Design, for the apron pattern that brought so much joy to my mother's last months. Aprons from her pattern are shown on both the cover and back of this book. Patterns can be purchased from: vanillahousedesigns.com

# About The Author

Gwen graduated from Carsonville High School in 1970, attended St. Clair County Community College in Port Huron, Michigan and graduated from the Alma Practical Nurse Center in Alma, Michigan in 1972. She attended Mesa State College in Grand Junction, Colorado, from 1987-1989. In 1992, she graduated Summa Cum Laude from the University of Utah with a Bachelor of Science degree. She continued her studies at the University of Utah pursuing a master's degree in Geography, but proved herself a quitter when dating Lon and playing with grandkids were a whole lot more fun than taking another statistics class. She ended a 10-year career with Salt Lake County as a Cartographer and Geographic Information Analyst to pursue a life of travel with her husband Lon.

Gwen and Lon still enjoy life without a mortgage and live anywhere they want—in campgrounds, on their sailboat, on BLM land in the West, and sometimes in the comfort of a *stationary* home with numerous friends.

For more stories and information, visit the author at:

alzheimerhumor.blogspot.com

Or email at:
aprons4alzheimers@gmail.com

All profits from sales of
*When Life Hands You Alzheimer's, Make Aprons!*
Go to Alzheimer's respite care

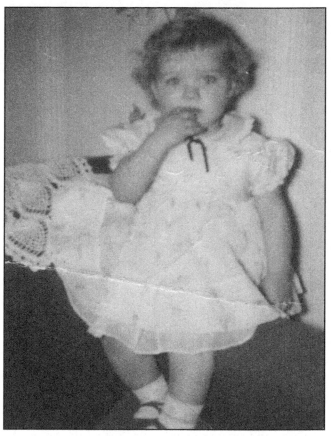

*Photo courtesy of the Katie Frostic collection*

"Hmm, I don't recognize this person."
The author, at about age one, in her only baby picture.

# Baby Bib Instructions

Trace pattern, then enlarge pattern on copy machine by 165%. Print 2 copies onto 81/2 x 14 paper so you have pattern for body of bib and bottom piece to make the bib complete.

Place pattern on fold of cotton fabric, cut 2 from coordinating fabric

Place bib liner on fold. Cut 1 from fleece, flannel or any piece of cotton fabric

Sandwich the three pieces together for sewing. Place one fabric right side **up**, then the bib liner (it can be right side up or wrong side up, it doesn't matter) place the last bib piece with right side **down**. Pin together.

Sew around all edges with a 1/4 inch seam. Leave a three-inch opening at the bottom.

Clip curves and turn right side out. Finger press the edges smooth, turn in the edges of the opening, pin, and press with iron.

Topstitch 1/8 inch around the edges.

Sew a snap on back of neck tabs.

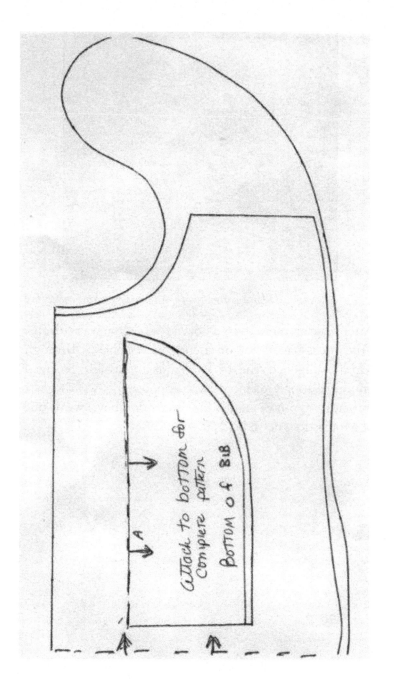

Attach to bottom for Complete pattern

Bottom of Bib

A

*Photo courtesy of the Connie Nelson collection*

After making more than a dozen bibs, Mom was curious, "You must have a lot of friends with babies." Through Mom's diligence, the little friends in my life received an ample supply of bibs. Zach (opposite) is wearing the miniature apron we made, his sister Zoe (above) wears one of Mom's designer bibs.

*Photo courtesy of the Connie Nelson collection*

CPSIA information can be obtained at www.ICGtesting.com
Printed in the USA
LVOW04s1629070115

421885LV00016B/607/P